TALKING ABOUT THE
END of DAYS

View of Our Times Based on Revealed & Inner Teachings of Torah

Thirtysix.org

Talking About the End of Days

View of Our Times Based on Revealed & Inner Teachings of Torah

ISBN 9781521943854

Published by:
Thirtysix.org
22 Yitzchak Road
Telzstone, Kiryat Yearim
Israel   90838

Rabbi Mordechai Friedlander
Rosh Kollel "Nechamas Yerushalayim"
23 Hoshea Street, Jerusalem

הרב מרדכי פרידלנדר
ראש הכולל "נחמת ירושלים"
23 רח' הושע, ירושלים

אור ליום כ"ח תמוז שנת התשס"ג לפ"ק פה ירושלים עה"ק תבב"א

שמחתי בראותי את ספרו של מע"כ ידידי אהוב לכל הרב המופלג בתו"ש מוה"ר פינחס
וינסטון, שליט"א, על העין החשוב של "אחרית הימים."

כבר עידן עידנין איתמחא גברא ואיתמחא קמיעא בספריו הנפלאים שזכה להוציא לאור
עולם ורבים מתחממים ונהנים מאורו. ועכשיו מתחכן להוסיף נדבך מעשה ידי אומן ומעשה
חושב עינים נחוצים העומדים על הפרק בפרקן של ישראל היקום מן שמיא שכולנו
מייחלים לה בבליון עינים בעגלא ובזמן קריב, אמן. הכל עשה יפה בעתו המחבר שליט"א
ביד ה' הטובה עליו ועם בשרון הגדיר אשר חונן בו בלע"ה מחשבות עמוקות וטהורות
וחשבונות עפ"י מדרשי חז"ל הק', הזוהר הק', וכ' האר"י הק' זיע"א, ועוד.

וכמתאים לח"ח וכן תורה מובהק הזוהר המחבר שליט"א בספרו כו"כ פעמים שודע
הקורא שאעפ"י שדבריו מיוסדים על יסודות הק' תג"ל ל"מ הרבדים הם בדרך אפשר
והחשבונות הם בדרך השערות טובות כי הוראות הלא אין אתנו יודע והדברים הם כמוסים
וחתומים עם הקל תמים רעות יתב"ש. אבל כן משמש הספר הצפוין הזה להלהבת
הלבבות ולזרז כלי המעשה ולהכין את עצמינו לקראת משיח צדקינו בתשובה שלימה.

הכותב והחותם לכבוד התורה ועמליה,

מרדכי פרידלנדר

הרב מרדכי פרידלנדר
רב ונמליץ ממון משמרת סתרים
ירושלים עהיי

THE CONCEPT OF *Moshiach* is both a simple and complicated one. The term itself is a Hebrew word meaning *"anointed one,"* since kings descending from the tribe of Yehudah were initiated by being anointed with special olive oil. Outside of the Jewish world, the word over time changed forms in different languages, and in English it is "messiah," which is used to refer to a "redeemer."

In his short but classic work, *The Thirteen Principles of Faith,* Maimonides, the *Rambam*, wrote:

> *I believe with perfect faith in the coming of Moshiach, and even though he may tarry, nevertheless, I will wait for him every day, that*

he will come.

The understanding of this twelfth principle of faith is clear: Jews have an obligation to believe that *Moshiach* could arrive any day, at any time.

One would think, based upon this directive, that believing Jews would live lives that take this idea into account. When something important in life is imminent, it usually occupies much of the daily discussion and plays a role in one's decision-making process.

However, for many Jews over the centuries, this has not necessarily been the case, and the following address to a small audience by Rabbi Yechezkel Levenstein, the *mashgiach* of the famed Mir Yeshivah in Poland (before World War II), and the Mir Yeshivah of Jerusalem and Ponovez (after the war), could easily have been addressed to much of the Jewish world:

> The *Sefer Mitzvos HaKatan*[1] wrote in his explanation of the positive *mitzvah* of, "*I am God, your God, Who took you out of Egypt*" (Shemos 20:2), that it means, one must know that He Who created Heaven and Earth alone controls [the world] above and below. He added, "This [*mitzvah*] is the basis for what the rabbis teach: 'At the time of a person's judgment after death

---

[1] Yitzchak ben Yosef of Corbeil (d.1280).

they ask him, 'Did you anticipate redemption?' " (*Shabbos* 31a). Where is this *mitzvah* written? Actually, it comes from this [same *verse*], and just as, "*I am God, your God, Who took you out of Egypt,*" means that we are expected to believe that God redeemed us from Egypt, it also means "...I also want you to believe that I, God your God, will gather you in and redeem you in mercy a second time." According to this, belief in the future redemption is...included in the first of the Ten Commandments. If we check ourselves, it seems we are very far from having faith in the future redemption...When it comes to the arrival of *Moshiach* and the resurrection of the dead we are silent, as if embarrassed to speak about them, as if we have given up them altogether. The words of the *Sefer Mitzvos HaKatan* should cause our hearts to tremble...and anyone who is not involved with these matters is far from having any true faith... (*Ohr Yechezkel, Emunas HaGeulah*, 1960; p. 287)

Indeed, the situation is quite backwards. For, even though the concept of a messianic redeemer originates in Judaism, it is others who picked up on this idea, who speak of the concept continuously, although they have created their own version of who messiah is.

And, in truth, this is one of the reasons why traditional Judaism has dropped the subject for the time being. The many distortions and abuse of the concept have left a bad taste in the mouths of Jews throughout the centuries, especially since for almost 2000 years the catholic and derivative churches tried to impose their concept of messiah at pain of death and torture.

However, there were also internal disturbances that created severe resistance to the concept of *Moshiach* and the End-of-Days. There was the Shabtai Tzvi debacle in Europe around the year 1650. Claiming to be THE *Moshiach* of the Jewish people, he successfully convinced masses of downtrodden Jews that the Final Redemption was close at hand. People sold their homes in distant lands and made travel arrangements to *Eretz Yisroel*, and even threatened hostile gentiles with revenge.

One cannot begin to imagine the psychological and political fallout that resulted when Shabtai Tzvi, given a choice of conversion to Islam or death by the Sultan of the Ottoman Empire, chose the former and converted. The ripple effects of this spiritual crisis for the Jewish people reach even until this day, and resulted in all kinds of resolutions to avoid such fiascoes in the future.

The *Haskalah* Movement, or so-called "Jewish Enlightenment," which came on the heels of the Shabtai Tzvi catastrophe,[2] only served to further bury the concept of Jewish messianism. Its motto being, "Be a cosmopolitan man in the street and a Jew in your home," the *Haskalah* dramatically moved away from Torah consciousness with the desire of embracing modern Western culture.

However, more recently, other familiar reasons have interfered with the Jewish connection to the concept of *Moshiach* and redemption. The general rule is, when Jews prosper materialistically in exile, the need for redemption and *Moshiach* dwindles. Indeed, the thought that *Moshiach* could come at any moment and signal the end of this fourth and final exile sends a chill up and down the back of many believing Jews.

There is even a joke to this effect:

Ya'akov was a simple but devoted Jew who never had time to learn much Torah, though he longed to. The best he could do while plying a meager living was listen attentively to the rabbi's *dvar Torah* each Shabbos morning after ser-

---

[2] Shabtai Tzvi (August 1, 1626—c. September 17, 1676) was a Sephardic ordained Rabbi, though of Romaniote origin and a kabbalist, active throughout the Ottoman Empire, who claimed to be the long-awaited *Moshiach*. He prove to be a false messiah, especially when he converted to Islam, causing much religious and political backlash.

vices. Then, he would return home to his wife and lovingly repeat the rabbi's wise words at Shabbos lunch.

However, one Shabbos, Ya'akov returned home white in the face and somewhat hysterical, and his wife was terribly concerned.

"Ya'akov!" she cried, *"What is the matter? What has happened to you?! You look like you've seen a ghost!"*

But, poor Ya'akov could only repeat over and over again, *"The rabbi . . . the rabbi . . . the rabbi . . ."*

"The rabbi what?" his wife tried to understand, *"Did something terrible happen to the rabbi, God forbid?"*

Ya'akov, finally calming down somewhat, answered his wife. *"No,"* he began. *"It is what the rabbi said today."*

"What could he have said that could shake you up like this?" she asked.

"He said . . . he said . . . that this Moshiach fellow is going to come soon, and we'll have to sell our houses and belongings and . . . and . . ."

"And WHAT?" his wife said, raising her voice in concern.

"AND MOVE TO ISRAEL!" Ya'akov blurted out as he put his face in his hands and cried, *"Oy,*

what will be!"

"Ya'akov," she said in a calming tone of voice. *"Ya'akov, calm down. It will be okay. You have to have faith! For, just like God saved our people from the Crusades and the Holocaust, He'll save us from Moshiach too!"*

If there were not a strong element of truth to the joke, it might be funny. However, instead of laughing, we have reason for grave concern. That so many Jews not only do not look for *Moshiach* daily, but rather fear that his coming will interfere with life as they know it, is the motivation for this book. It is a compilation of sources and ideas that show us how crucial the concept and reality of *Moshiach* is to our lives and our very survival as Jewish individuals and as the Jewish nation in our given role as the *"light unto nations."*

Talking About
the End-of-Days

THE TOPIC OF the *End-Of-Days*, as mentioned already, is a touchy one. Therefore, before going any further, it is important to answer some of the more prevalent questions that arise when discussing this subject.

QUESTION #1: Is it permissible to speak about the "End-of-Days," namely, the "Days of *Moshiach*"?

The truth is, many, many sources *do*, including the Talmud (see *Sanhedrin* 97a-99a). Countless other books have been written solely on this subject over the generations by very respected rabbis. More recently, the book *When Moshiach Comes: Halachic and Aggadic Perspectives,* was published (1994), an English version of the Hebrew work, *Otzros Acharis HaYomim,* by Rabbi Yehudah Chayoun.[1]

QUESTION #2: What then *is* forbidden regarding discussing the End-of-Days?

The Talmud states:

Rav Shmuel ben Nachmani said in the name of Rav Yonason: May the spirit of those who calculate the end expire. For, they say, "Since the predetermined time has arrived and [*Moshiach*] has yet to come, he will never come!" (*Sanhedrin* 97b)

Whoever forecasts the date of *Moshiach's* arrival has no place in the World-to-Come. (*Meseches Derech Eretz* 11)

Hence, we see that the Talmud is only concerned about making *calculations* regarding the pre-

---

[1] Approbations are from *gedolim* such as, Rabbi Shlomo Zalman Auerbach, *zt"l*, Rabbi Shalom Eliyashiv, *shlita*, Rabbi Shmuel HaLevi Wosner, *shlita*, Rabbi Chaim Pinchas Scheinberg, *shlita*, Rabbi Chaim Kenievsky, *shlita*, and Rabbi Aharon Leib Shteinman, *shlita*.

cise day for *Moshiach's* arrival, since errors in such calculations usually result in national disappointment, and perhaps, revelations of false messiahs. The *Rambam* mentions this in his introduction to *"Chelek,"* the eleventh chapter of *Sanhedrin*, where he writes: "One should not assign a date and explain verses homiletically in order to pinpoint the date of *Moshiach's* arrival."

Furthermore, the Talmud wrote:

> When Rav Zeira happened upon scholars who were engaged [in calculating the date of the coming of *Moshiach*], he told them, "I beg you, do not postpone it…for it has been taught, 'Three things come when the mind is occupied otherwise: *Moshiach, something that is lost, and a scorpion.'* "(*Sanhedrin* 97a)

Additionally, there is also the concern that believing in a specific date will prevent a person from expecting *Moshiach* earlier than that date, a violation of the principle of "anticipating him *any* day." Failure to anticipate the possible arrival of *Moshiach* at any time, says the *Rambam*, can give such a Jew the *halachic* status of a heretic.[2]

---

2 *Hilchos Melachim* 11:1.

QUESTION #3: Yet, we see that great rabbis over the ages did precisely that, and were not chastised for doing so?

This is because the prohibition of calculating the arrival date of *Moshiach* has been interpreted differently by many rabbis, to name a few:

Ramban (1194-1270): The prohibition of the Talmud only applied to earlier generations; now that we are on the eve of redemption, there is no prohibition (*Sefer HaGeulah, Ma'amer 4*).

Zohar (1380): It is not God's will that the date of *Moshiach's* arrival be revealed to man, but when the date draws near, even children will be able to make the calculation (*Bereishis* 118a).

Abarbanel (1437-1508): It is forbidden to make the calculation based upon astrology; however, it is permissible to calculate a date based upon *Tanach* (*Maayeni HaYeshuah* 1:2).

Vilna Gaon (1720-1797): From here [what I have just written] you can calculate the time of the Final Redemption if, God forbid, we do not merit [to bring it earlier]; however, I have imposed an oath, in the name of the God of Israel, on the reader of this that he should not reveal it. (*Biur HaGR"A, Sifra D'Tzniusa*, Chapter Five)

Malbim (1809-1879): The situation is like that of a father and son traveling a long distance. As they start out, the son begins to ask when they will arrive, and of course, the father does not answer. However, as they near the town, the son asks the same question, and this time the father readily answers that it is only a short while before they reach their destination. So too it is with us: now that the time is clearly approaching, we cannot help but notice and interpret the signs all around us that tell of the impending *geulah* . . . As the time of the *keitz* grows nearer, the doubts will become smaller, and at the *keitz*, all doubts will be removed . . . As the time grows closer, the uncertainty recedes in the wake of the increasingly "abounding wisdom." (Introduction to *Daniel*)[3]

---

[3] There is a similar parable told over in the name of the Dubno Maggid, which ends: "Father," the son later asked, "you told me before not to ask such questions." The father answered, "My son, before we were far from our destination, so it was not worthwhile to discuss the issue. But now that we are close, we must know exactly when we will arrive in order to prepare ourselves."

QUESTION #4: What importance, if any, is there to speak about redemption and the End-of-Days?

The Talmud states:

Rava said: When they bring a person for judgment, they will say to him, "Did you deal faithfully in business? Did you set aside fixed times for Torah study? Did you try to have children? Did you anticipate the redemption?" (*Shabbos* 31a)

Assuredly, this does not mean ignoring the concept of *geulah*, even for the sake of other *mitzvos*, like the all-important *mitzvah* of learning Torah. On the contrary, the learning of Torah should only make one anticipate *geulah* that much more, the same way it should enhance one's love of *Eretz Yisroel*, and yearning to live there.

Furthermore, Rabbi Eliyahu Lopian, *zt"l*, wrote in the name of Rav Elchanan Wasserman, *zt"l*, the following:

I heard in London from the holy Rabbi Elchanan Wasserman, quoting the Chofetz Chaim, that *Chazal* say the war of Gog and Magog will be threefold. After the First World War, the Chofetz Chaim said that this was the first battle of Gog and Magog, and in about twenty-five years (1942) there would be a second world war, which would make the first one seem insignificant, and then there would be a third battle . . . Rav Elchanan concluded that one must suffer the pangs of *Moshiach*, but the wise man will quietly prepare himself during that time—perhaps he will be worthy of seeing the comforting of *Tzion* and *Yerushalayim*. (*Leiv Eliyahu, Shemos,* page 172)

There are many other sources to this effect, all of which serve to strengthen the point. As well, there are the numerous stories of pre-World War II Torah giants (such as the Chofetz Chaim), and how they lived with the daily reality of an imminent redemption. The following, perhaps, sums up what is lacking from our generation, which, *ironically*, lives so *close* to the Final Redemption:

If I could find more colleagues who felt the same . . .we would go out into the fields and demand with prayer and supplication and not return home until the Jewish people received eternal salvation and redemption through the coming of *Moshiach Ben Dovid.* (*Divrei Chaim of Sanz, Beis Shlomo*)

And, in the words of the great Chofetz Chaim himself:

Several times a day we request redemption, but requesting is not enough. We must *DEMAND* redemption, just as a worker demands his salary. For, the *halachah* is that if he does not, his employer need not pay him that day. (Commentary on the *Siddur*, section 168)

Finally, the Vilna Gaon put the concept of redemption in these terms, as told by his student:

The purpose of redemption is the true redemption and sanctification of God's Name. According to the words of our prophets and the explanation of our teacher (*Vilna Gaon*), the goal of our work is the war against Armelius,[4] carried out through the ingathering of the exiles and settling of the Land for the sake of the true redemption and sanctification of God's Name...We don't need to reach the appointed time (*moed*), but rather, the *moed* will come to us—after *"Your servants have cherished her stones and favor her dust"* (*Tehillim* 102:14-15)...The arrival of the Redeemer depends upon the building of

---

[4] The Ministering Angel that represents the *Erev Rav* in Heaven.

Tzion. (*Kol HaTor*, Chapter 4:1-3)

Dealing With Historical Discrepancy

two

IT'S KIND OF par for the course. As if there wasn't already enough confusion concerning Judaism and Torah, there is a historical discrepancy as well. And, as is usually the case in the minds of the masses when it comes to Judaism versus the Western world, the Torah viewpoint is considered secondary to Western opinion—even, in this case, according to some Orthodox Jews.

We are talking about a discrepancy of 167 years, to be exact, which, in the course of 6,000 years is not that much time. However, when it comes to placing key historical dates in their proper historical context, it is a *huge* amount of time with which to err. Some prominent examples include:

Event	Jewish	Western
1st Temple Destroyed	423 BCE	590 BCE
Cyrus conquers Babylonia	371 BCE	538 BCE
2nd Temple Construction	353 BCE	520 BCE

The entire Second Temple period was 420 years.[1] By the time it was destroyed—70 CE—Western dating became more accurate, around the time of Josephus. However, until that time, nations thought they ruled forever, and history was more propaganda than a record of true events.

In the meantime, the Jewish people have been keeping track of time ever since God first told Moshe while still in Egypt:

This month shall be for you the beginning of the months, it shall be for you the first of the months of the year. (Shemos 12:2)

This wasn't just a *mitzvah* to sanctify the new moon each month; it was God handing over to man, specifically the Jewish people, the responsibility of keeping track of the years from that point onward.

Rabbi Sa'adiah Gaon states that traditional

---

[1] *Seder Olam*, Chapter 30; *Arachin* 12b.

chronology is indisputably supported by *Tanach*.[2] Rabbi Ya'akov Emden, in his glosses to *Seder Olam* wrote:

> Those who assume that the Second Temple stood longer than 420 years are forced to contradict the simple meaning of Scripture.

Which, of course, we do not do. However, if one counts backwards from the year 70 CE, the accepted year of the destruction of the Second Temple, one does not arrive at the Western date for its construction. Other sources to this effect include the *Maharal*,[3] and *Igros Chazon Ish*.[4]

Certainly, when talking about the End-of-Days, a 167-year time discrepancy can shift the period right out of someone's lifetime. Therefore, it is important to this discussion to explain some of the background behind the Torah dating system.

Traditional Jewish chronology is based upon dating as found in *Seder Olam*, an authoritative work dating back to Talmudic times (5 CE), and the Talmud itself. *Seder Olam* is based upon an UNINTERRUPTED tradition of Torah and rabbinical sources, and was the

---

[2] *Emunos v'Dayos,* end of M. 8.
[3] *Be'er HaGolah*, 6.
[4] Part 1, 206.

basis for calculating such *halachic* realities as *Shmittah* years.

However, as mentioned above, the Western dating system with which we are presently familiar was non-existent in ancient times. In such early times, events were dated from the time a new king assumed the throne, often as if the world had been created all over again. History was often fabricated to justify the king's rise to the throne and his rule.[5]

Indeed, history in ancient times, for the most part, was a propaganda tool in the hands of the present ruling autocracy, adjusted to suit the will of the existing rulership, and imposed upon its country-men and history. For this reason, much of history through the eyes of the modern Western world is calculated retroactively, leaving much room for gaping discrepancies and inaccuracies.[6]

As well, it must be noted and appreciated that ancient secular documents were never as scrupulously preserved by so many God-fearing people, or so many nations for that matter, as was *Tanach*, *Seder Olam*, and the *Talmud*.

It can also be pointed out that when it comes to

---

[5] In recent times, Nazi Germany and Stalinist Russia did the exact same thing.

[6] For a complete discussion of this issue, see the *History of the Jewish People: The Second Temple Era*; Mesorah Publications, 1982; pp. 211-214.

traditional Jewish historians, going back to the time of the *Geonim* (589-1038 CE), the *Rishonim* (1038-1501 CE), and forward until present-day, the Jewish date is taken to be accurate. For example, Kabbalists such as the *Ramban* (1194-1270 CE) predicted dates for the arrival of *Moshiach* based upon Kabbalah—which would have been irrelevant if the Jewish date was inaccurate.

This is true of many others before and after the *Ramban*. Furthermore, none even address the possibility of Jewish historical inaccuracy, seemingly because they were confident in the ability of previous Torah generations to accurately keep track of time, dates, and events.

There is one very crucial reason why: because belief in God's involvement in the affairs of the Jewish people (*Hashgochah Pratis*) makes the date and timing of an event meaningful and insightful in itself, and therefore, worthy of accurate and precise recording. This can hardly be said of Western dating, which believes in a randomly evolving history.

For example, the First Temple was destroyed in the Jewish year 3338, which, when written in its corresponding Hebrew letters, *Shin-Lamed-Ches*, spells the Hebrew word *"shlach."* The word itself means "send," and is an allusion to the "sending" of the Jewish people into Babylonian exile.

Another example of the confidence of the great

rabbis of the past in the existing Hebrew chronology comes later in history, and from the following quote:

> Heard from our teacher *HaRav* Chaim from Volozhin is that the *GR"A* (Vilna Gaon) said that the book *"Mishnah Torah"* (*Devarim*) in each *parsha* alludes to what will happen in each one hundred years of the sixth millennium—ten *parshios* corresponding to ten periods of one hundred years each.[7] Rav Chaim asked him, "Where are we hinted to in *Parashas Ki Seitzei?"*[8] He answered him that his (the *GR"A's*) name was hinted to in the words *"evven shlaimah"* (*Devarim* 25:15). (*Sefer HaEmunah v'HaHashgochah*)

The words mean, "complete stone," necessary for the accurate weights and measures the Torah expects us to use when doing business. However, the word *"shlaimah"* can also be read "Shlomo," the name of the Vilna Gaon's father. The word *"evven"* can be read *"Aleph, Bais-Nun,"* with the *Aleph* referring to the

---

[7] *Nitzavim* and *Vayailech* are almost always read together on one Shabbos, and are therefore considered to be like a single *parashah*.

[8] Which corresponded to the 100-year period 5500-5600/1740-1840 CE, in which they had lived.

first letter of his name, "Eliyahu."[9]

Would the Vilna Gaon have made the comparison if the date 5500 was off by 167 years? He would have been living in a period that corresponded to a different *parsha* altogether! And, he held that the allusion to his name, followed by the account of Amalek at the end of the *parsha*, which was followed by a discussion about *Eretz Yisroel* and its produce, was an allusion to the sequence of events leading up to the Final Redemption.[10]

Furthermore, there is a tradition that every verse in the Torah corresponds to a year of history since Creation. For example, the 5,698th *verse*[11] reads as follows:

> *God was angered and brought upon you all the curses written here. (Devarim* 29:26)

The Hebrew year 5698, when written out in Hebrew letters, spells the Hebrew word, *"tirtzach"* which means, "you will murder." As it works out, the year 5698 corresponds to the Western year 1938—the year

---

[9] When asked why only the first letter from his name was revealed, he answered, "Because it was known that I would only reveal part of the Torah I learned."

[10] *Kol HaTor.*

[11] *Parashas Ki Savo.*

of the infamous "Kristallnacht Pogrom" in Germany, and the beginning of what would eventually be Hitler's "Final Solution"—the Holocaust—to what he called "The Jewish Problem."

This correlation would be meaningless if the Jewish year "5698" did not correspond to the Western year 1938, and yet it is made and supported with hints from the *Zohar* itself. And, there are many similar examples to show that traditional Judaism abides by its current date as being accurate since Creation, and many reasons to assume that it is correct in its understanding.

Why 6000 Years

THIS YEAR, ACCORDING to the Jewish calendar, is 5763 *from Creation*. However, to millions of Jews it means little more than 3763, 4763, or 6763, and to many, all that really counts is that it is the year 2003 according to the Western dating system.

Then comes the news: *history as we know it will only last 6000 years.*

Simple math reveals that there are only 237 years left. It's still enough to live a few lifetimes at our present rate of life expectancy, but it does serve to provide somewhat of a jolt. Compared to estimates of 4 billion years, 237 years is "just around the corner."

Before we get to the serious part about history coming to an end LONG before that, the question arises, "Why 6000 years?" Where did that number come from?

To begin with, it is in the Talmud:

> For 6,000 years the world will exist, and for one [thousand years] it will be destroyed. (*Sanhedrin* 97a)

Noteworthy is that no one argues with the above statement in the Talmud; it seems to be taken as fact. *Rashi* doesn't even bother to explain what the Talmud means by this statement, a clear indication that the 6000 years is to be taken *literally*.

The *Ramchal[1]* concurs:

> The entire world must similarly be destroyed, and then renewed. This is the meaning of what our rabbis have taught, "For 6000 years the world will exist, and for one [thousand years] it will be destroyed." (*Sanhedrin* 97a). At the end of this 1000 years, God will again renew His world. (*Derech Hashem*, 1:3:9)

According to the *Rambam,* however, it is not so simple. Apparently, the *Rambam* held that the Talmud's statement was not unanimous, but only expres-

---

[1] Rabbi Chaim Moshe Luzzatto, 1770-1746 CE.

sive of one opinion and therefore it is not to be taken literally.[2]

However, just about everyone else with an opinion on the matter disagrees with the *Rambam*, especially the Kabbalists, including the *Ra'avad*, who took the *Rambam* to task for contradicting the Talmud.[3] The reason for the difference of opinion may be the fact that:

> The *Rambam* was from the "Left *Pe'ah*"[4] [in the *sefiros*] and therefore he did not merit to learn the wisdom of the *Zohar*. The *Ramban* was from the "Right *Pe'ah*," and therefore he *did* merit to learn it, as is known. (*Sha'ar HaG- ilgulim*, Chapter 36)

In fact:

> Anyone who learns *Kabbalah* causes a great *tikun* and revelation of the light of His Holy Name...After Moshe received it from God, it was handed down from person to person, just to the select few of each generation. During the

---

[2] *Moreh Nevuchim* 2:29.

[3] *Yad, Teshuvah* 8:8.

[4] The hair that grows downward in front of the ear to the cheekbone.

time of the *Geonim* (589-1038 CE), everything was hidden until the time of the *Ramban* (1194-1270 CE), in whose generation the *Zohar* was revealed (1380 CE). Later, through the great light of the *Arizal*, all portions of the *Nistar* (Hidden Torah) were revealed. (*Drushei Olam HaTohu* 1:113b)

And, as we shall see, the number "6000" can *only* be understood within the context of Kabbalah, as the Vilna Gaon (1720-1779 CE) explained:

Know that each day of Creation alludes to a thousand years of our existence, and every little detail that occurred on these days will have its corresponding event happen at the proportionate time during its millennium. (*Sifra D'Tzniusa*, Chapter Five)

In fact, this idea that one millennium of history corresponds to one day of Creation is taken so literally that it is said that one hour during the six days of Creation corresponds to 83.33 years within the corresponding millennium.[5] And, this relationship of one day to 1000 years is echoed in *Tehillim*—

---

[5] *Pirkei d'Rebi Eliezer* 48.

For one thousand years in Your eyes are but a day that has passed. (Tehillim 90:4)

Kabbalah explains why:

All the forces of *Gevuros* are rooted in the SIX *sefiros—Chesed, Gevurah, Tifferes, Netzach, Hod, Yesod*—which are the SIX days of Creation, and also the SIX thousand years of history that the world will exist. And, within them (the six *sefiros*) are the roots of all that will happen from the six days of Creation until the Final Rectification. (*Drushei Olam HaTohu* 2:151b)

What's a *sefirah*? There are many ways to discuss the *Sefiros* and their function in Creation. However, in this respect, they are being understood as the spiritual "DNA" of the six days of Creation, and the six millennia that have followed since then. As the *Ramchal* taught:

The second concept involves the fact that every single day of the six thousand years has its own separate decree from God. (*Derech Hashem* 4:4:11)

In other words, though the days of our lives may seem somewhat random and without any real significance, just a chain of time moving on endlessly, it is not anymore true than why a person's hair turns gray at a specific point in his life. Our lives are the result of a genetic "script," and the parts of our body respond to internal instructions recorded before we were even born.

Thus, for each millennium there is a corresponding *sefirah*, which is, for all intents and purposes, the cosmic "script" for that particular millennium— *Chesed* for the first 1000 years, *Gevurah* for the second 1000 years, and so on until we arrive at *our* millennium, which is governed by the *sefirah* called "*Yesod.*" It has been decreed that each *sefirah* govern exactly 1000 years, *no more and no less*.

Think of it in terms of a computer. People often play with computers, unaware of what their actions may cause. However, whatever the result, it is the consequence of a program that is the computer's instructions on how to respond to specific causes, buried deep within the "brains" of the computer itself.

The *sefiros* are the "brains" of Creation, except that they are really just expressions of the Divine will and instruments for implementing it. However different the sixth millennium is from the fifth, it is because *Yesod* is different from *Hod*, the *sefirah* that governed that millennium. It was a different set of instructions unique for that period of 1000 years, because that is what God decreed was best for that time period in terms of the ultimate goal of Creation and the development of man.

Therefore, why 6000 years? Because, the 6000 years are rooted in the *six* days of Creation, like trees are rooted in the tiny little seeds from which they originally sprouted. And, the six days of Creation are rooted in the six *sefiros* of *Chesed* through *Yesod*, each of which governs a period of time equal to exactly 1000 years, man-time.

It is precise, which means there really *are* only 237 years of history left as we know it. And, it is not exactly 237 years left of history as we know it either, as we will discuss in the next chapter, *b'ezras Hashem*.

Of Predictions
& Prophecies

four

ANTI-SEMITISM IS BACK, and with a vengeance. And yet, it seems that just a short time ago the world had outgrown anti-Semitism. *What changed?*

The truth is, a student of Jewish history has to notice a trend that can and should make every Jew nervous. It appears that most "golden eras" that the Jewish People enjoy while living in *"Chutz L'Aretz"*[1]— such as the one we are presently enjoying in places like America, Canada, England, South Africa, etc.—do not usually last more than fifty or so years before coming to an unexpected and undesirable end.

Indeed, it seems as if no matter where Jews set-

---

[1] Literally, "outside the Land," or the Diaspora.

tle down or what they do, [2] the exile of any particular time usually ends the same way: with virulent anti-Semitism and rejection of the local Jewish population. This has been true even in countries where Jews were initially greeted with compassion; somehow, over time, we always tend to wear out the welcome.

In truth, this is not a mystery—if one believes, as the Talmud teaches, that anti-Semitism is supernatural,[3] a means employed by God to transmit to the Jewish People messages such as, *"It is time to move on."* Anti-Semitism seems to be a *last resort*[4] form of Heavenly communication to remind us that we do not belong anywhere permanently except in *Eretz Yisroel*—something that is difficult to recall while being part of productive and open gentile societies.

Therefore, it has seemed for some time now, that the sanctuary the Jewish People currently enjoy amongst the nations of the world is bound to come to an end, perhaps even an abrupt one. *To an end*, because so many decades have already passed without stirrings from Heaven, and *abruptly*, because Jews (including the Orthodox) seem overly attached to

---

[2] Even, and *often* in places where Jews are the most assimilated and the least Jewishly visible, anti-Semitism is rampant.

[3] *Shabbos* 89a.

[4] Like any loving parent, God also gives early and gentle warnings which, if obeyed, end the need for more drastic ones, such as anti-Semitism.

their foreign lands.

And, like clockwork, all of a sudden, anti-Semitism is back, and getting worse. Though, at first, it seemed as if there were only anti-Israel sentiments because of Israeli reluctance to accept a Palestinian state, in the end, it has become clear that anti-Israelism is just another form of anti-Semitism. (Heaven is less concerned about the form of Anti-Semitism than it is about its effect on the Jewish psyche.)

One thing that we Jews did not count on was the spread of Islam to the rest of the world, and the introduction of large numbers of Arabs into Western populations; and while the typical American may not be likely or even capable of carrying out terrorist attacks on local Jewish populations, the Wahabbi Islam—practicing Arab communities that have moved in "next door" are. Never by Americans, perhaps, but, "Never in America!" is another story today.[5]

Indeed, in this light, one must ask: Was September 11, 2001, the destruction of the World Trade Center by Arab terrorists, an initial step in the process of loosening the Jewish hold on *Chutz L'Aretz?* The attack has certainly left many American Jews feeling

---

[5] Heaven uses many messengers, both those with good and those with evil intent, to do whatever the Highest Wisdom deems necessary to wake the Jewish people up from its long slumber in exile.

less secure; some even made *aliyah* as a result, while others were "forced" to actually consider the idea for the first time in their lives.

However, prior to September 11, Jews balked. It was hard for us to believe that America the "secure" could ever have anything happen to it on so large a scale as the complete destruction of the Twin Towers. Perhaps it could happen in Israel, we thought, but not in America. And, as far as Europe was concerned, we reasoned, Europeans seemed to have moved past their anti-Semitic ways.

And, this is the way many tend to feel—until they consider the 6000-year timeline.

At first, it is a new idea for many to learn that the Talmud only allows for 6000 years of history.[6] After hearing for so long that the world has 4 billion years left to go until the sun dies in a supernova, 6000 years seems, well, kind of imminent. Hearing about the 6000 years tends to give people reason to pause once they see how close history, and reality as we know it, is rapidly coming to its "end" on the timeline.

"But why only 6,000 years?" people ask.

The Talmud does not explain itself, but instead leaves that to Kabbalah to reveal.[7] And, while explaining that, Kabbalistic tradition also reveals that the six

---

[6] *Sanhedrin* 97a.
[7] See the previous chapter, *"Why 6000 Years?"*

thousand years actually correspond to the six days of Creation, making them the basis for all that has happened throughout history, and will happen during the remainder of the 6000 years.[8]

The urgency of this idea becomes clearer when one divides 1000 (years) by a factor 12,[9] in order to calculate what one hour of Creation equals in a millennium: 83.33 years. And, if history since the expulsion from the Garden of Eden has been for the sake of rectifying the sin of Adam *HaRishon*, which it has been, then we need to know what period of history corresponds to the hour during which he ate from the Tree of Knowledge of Good and Evil.

For, it is reasonable to assume that, if the six days of Creation are the basis for all that occurs throughout the six millennia—

> Know that each day of Creation alludes to a thousand years of our existence, and every little detail that occurred on these days will have its corresponding event happen at the proportion-

---

[8] It is actually quite fascinating to see how events that have occurred over the millennia can actually be related to events that occurred during the six days of creation, at the corresponding time.

[9] According to *Pirkei d'Rebi Eliezer* (48), we divide by 12 since God only created during the daytime hours, and night was "absorbed" into the 12 daytime hours.

ate time during its millennium. (*Sifra D'Tzniusa*, Chapter Five)

—then there will come a time in the future that will repeat, on some level, the challenge the First Man underwent, and failed. There will come an 83.33-year period of time that will correspond to the hour on Day Six during which Adam made his fateful error, for which we still pay until this very day.

And, when that period of time finally comes, the generation living at that time, it is logical to assume, will confront a similar challenge that Adam *HaRishon* did, with an opportunity to rectify the sin. For all we know, it will not be just another test in the history of mankind, but *THE* test of history, perhaps even corresponding to the last possible time for *Moshiach* to arrive.

Now, according to the Talmud, Adam *HaRishon* ate from the Tree of Knowledge of Good and Evil during the tenth hour of Day Six (*Sanhedrin* 38b). Based upon the calculation mentioned above, we arrive at the following table:

	Jewish Date	Western Date
1	5000—5083	1240—1323 CE
2	5084—5167	1324—1407
3	5168—5250	1408—1490
4	5251—5333	1491—1573

5	5334–5417	1574–1657
6	5318–5500	1658–1740
7	5501–5583	1741–1823
8	5584–5667	1824–1907
9	5668–5750	1908–1990
10	5751–5833	1991–2073
11	5834–5917	2074–2157
12	5918–6000	2158–2240

Thus, it turns out that in the Western year 1991, the period that corresponds to the tenth hour of Day Six began. If so, then the question becomes, what occurred around 1991 that can be traced back to the Tree of Knowledge of Good and Evil, at least conceptually? What, if anything, is a modern version of the Tree of Knowledge of Good and Evil?

Fascinatingly, there was a major technological breakthrough at that time that has since dominated the world's attention, for better or for worse, and that was the Internet. Coincidentally, it was precisely around that time that it burst on to the international scene, dramatically transforming man's access to knowledge and his use of it.

It did not take long to realize the potential good of the Internet. Even the Torah world got involved early with the Internet to advance the cause of spreading Torah and expanding the arm of outreach. The Internet proved to truly be a "super information highway."

However, at the same time, the side of evil also realized the potential of the Internet to enhance access to even greater levels of immorality and destruction. For one, the Internet, by virtue of its ease of access, removed many of the barriers that often protected the innocent from the world of indecency. It also provides easier access to even greater means of societal destruction, like bombs for example.

A tree of knowledge? *For sure.* Of good? *Absolutely.* Of evil? *Seems so*, as even those from the Western world advise caution and restraint when allowing access to the Internet. Is the Internet a modern, technological, Tree of Knowledge of Good and Evil? It certainly represents a major test for mankind.

However, 1991 was only the beginning of the 83.33-year period of time that corresponds to the tenth hour of Day Six. As of the writing of this article, it is only 2003, which means that another 71.33 years still remain in this period of time, during which so much can happen that might better resemble the First Man's test.

Not necessarily, as the following reveals:

As a result, the period of resurrection for the entire generation will be long, though *tzaddikim* who have died previously will resurrect immediately at the beginning of the period—forty years after the ingathering of the exiles.

This is what it says in the Midrash: There will be many resurrections, and the period of time will continue, according to Rebi Yehudah from forty years after *Kibbutz Golios*, at which time the first resurrection will occur, and continue until the last resurrection, a period of 210 years. Rebi Yitzchak says: 214 years. (*Drushei Olam HaTohu, Chelek 2, Drush 4, Anaf 12, Siman 9*)

If this is true, then it turns out that the 71.33 remaining years of the "tenth hour" of the sixth millennium was just reduced by 44.33 years. For, according to the *Zohar's* calculation, *Techiyas HaMeisim*—Resurrection of the Dead, when bodies are recreated and reunited with their souls, is destined to begin at least 210 years *BEFORE* the year 6000, in the year 2030 CE!

And that, says the *Zohar*, is only after 40 years of *Kibbutz Golios*—ingathering of the Jews to *Eretz Yisroel*. Based upon this calculation, the actual ingathering of the exiles back to *Eretz Yisroel* from the "four corners of the earth" would have begun sometime between 1986 and 1990. Does this not change the way we look at recent and current events?

For example, Russia, the last country to hold Jews against their will in great numbers, all of a sudden imploded at the end of the 1980s. Why, and why then? Most historians are not quite sure, but one thing we know for certain is that it resulted in a complete reversal of Soviet emigration policy, opening the door to Jewish emigration.

It was also around this time that "Operation Moses" took place. This was a daring airlift by the Israeli air force to bring home to Israel a large number of Ethiopians who claimed to be of Jewish descent. Just another momentous event in the modern state of Israel's short history, or part of a larger master plan for the Jewish people that is beginning to reach its inevitable and promised conclusion?

The excitement did not end there. In the year 1998, something else began to make headlines: Y2K, otherwise known as the "Millennium Bug." Something as simple and seemingly insignificant as the changing of the date from 1999 to 2000 threatened to cause major havoc worldwide through millions of computers incapable of making the transition.

And, as if to thicken the plot, two predictions by great rabbis of the past all of a sudden surfaced regarding the year 5760, which just happened to coincide with Year 2000. Both the *Rokayach* (1160-1237 CE) and the *Chesed L'Avraha*m (1558-1646 CE) had written hundreds of years ago that in the year 5760 a major "flood" would occur, drowning the evil and saving the righteous.

A flood of *what?* Of *water?*

All of a sudden, some wondered if the flood was to be one of international chaos instead: was Y2K destined to be the instrument of destruction?

Dovid *HaMelech* once wrote:

This is from God, that which is wondrous in our eyes. (Tehillim 118:23)

In other words, Dovid *HaMelech* was saying, if something seems out of the ordinary, especially when it comes to Jewish history, it is to be taken as a sign from Heaven. Without prophets, we have little to tell us what God is up to, and what to expect next. If we accept the notion of *Hashgochah Pratis*, of individual Divine Providence, then we have to accept that God uses history as a means of communication as well. But how?

Dovid *HaMelech* answered this question by explaining that God makes events occur out of the ordinary, in order to catch our attention and tell us a little about what's on His mind. Y2K was certainly such an event, consuming tens of thousands of hours of thinking time, tons of newsprint, and creating panic amongst the masses. When all was said and done, the world spent some 64 billion dollars to avert the anticipated crisis.

As it turned out, 5760/2000 CE happened to also be the sixth year of that *Shmittah* Cycle. The Talmud writes:

The rabbis taught: [Concerning] the seven-year cycle after which *Moshiach* will come, in the first year the verse, *"I caused it to rain on one city, but, on another city, I did not cause it to rain"* (*Amos* 4:7) [will be fulfilled]. In the second year, [there will be] slight famine (*Rashi:* a slight famine so that no place will be completely satisfied). In the third year, the famine will be great and men, women, children, pious people, and men of good deeds will die; Torah will be forgotten by those who learned it. In the fourth year, some will be satiated while others are not, but in the fifth year there will be plenty and people will eat, drink, and be joyous and Torah will return to those who learned it. In the sixth year, there will be voices (*Rashi:* people will speak of *Moshiach's* imminent arrival or the shofar announcing his arrival will be heard). In the seventh year, there will be war. *Motzei Shvi'is*, Ben Dovid will come. Rav Yosef said, "Many seven(-year cycles) have come and still he did not come." Abaye answered, "Were there voices in the sixth year and was there war in the seventh?" (*Sanhedrin* 97a)

As a result of Y2K, a good portion of the world became quite messianic, and it spilled over into the Jewish world as well. It was just all too coincidental.

Then came September 11, 2001, and the unexpected and shocking terrorist attack against the World Trade Center in New York. Against all the odds and after just a few hours, two hijacked jetliners caused the death of about 3,000 people, obliterated a major symbol of American security and prowess, and sent the world into a tailspin from which it has yet to recover.

It had been the seventh year of the *Shmittah* cycle, and sure enough, war was declared and war had begun.

In fact, the Americans actually began their retaliation just after Hoshanah Rabbah began in *Eretz Yisroel*, in 5762, the eighth year of the *Shmittah* cycle, only one year after the second Intifada had begun in Israel. That too had caught the Israelis and the world by surprise, just as Israel had made major concessions to the Palestinians for the sake of peace.

> Why did they make the blessing for redemption the seventh [one in the *Shemonah Esrai*]? Rava said, "Since [the Jewish people] are destined to be redeemed in the seventh [year of a *Shmittah* cycle], they made it the seventh [blessing]." But the master said, "In the sixth year there will be voices, in the seventh year war, and *Motzei Shvi'is* Ben Dovid will come" (*Sanhedrin* 97a). [Rava answered:] "War is also the beginning of the redemption." (*Megillah* 17b)

Well, war had begun; had the redemption begun too?

With such a historical picture forming, it was difficult not to suspect something major was happening. To what extent it is difficult to know, but since then, another war has been fought in Iraq, the Israelis are being cajoled into a precarious peace plan, Anti-Semitism continues to worsen, and world security seems to be weakening on a daily basis.

To simply dismiss all the events and information as just another passing phase of history is not only illogical, it is downright irresponsible.

A computer is only as smart as its data base and its ability to access that information. Human beings are not much different. Yet, how many of us hurry to deepen our knowledge of Torah, beyond simply knowing what to do in everyday life situations? How many have taken the time to properly build a "big picture" of history through the eyes of Torah, to understand the mysterious undercurrents of Jewish history?

Today, as a people, we are asleep. Haman noticed this in his time and tried to take advantage of it. Had not God made sure that at least one Mordechai was alive then, Haman would have realized his "final solution" for the Jewish people of that time. And now, though we can see it for ourselves in our time, we still go about business as usual, as if nothing much is out of place.

That the world has become less stable and Jews have become reviled once again is not the surprise. The REAL surprise today is just how deeply we can sleep with all that "racket" taking place around us. Like Yonah the prophet, we sleep soundly in the hold of our "ship," while our fellow crew members work frantically to keep the ship from succumbing to the storm.

What will happen next? What is the prediction? What does prophecy say?

These are all good questions. However, though Jewish history may indeed be supernatural, the answers to these questions need not be. God gave us a Torah, and with it tremendous insight into Creation, why He made it, and what He expects from Man, and particularly the Jewish people.

As the *Zohar* says:

> [Then] the men of understanding will know, because they are from the side of [the eighth *sefirah* called] *Binah*, which is the "Tree of Life." Of them it says, *"The Maskilim will emanate light like the light of the sky"* (Daniel 12:3)... with this work of yours, *Sefer HaZohar,* which is from the light of *Binah*, which is called *"teshuvah."* In the future *Yisroel* will taste from the "Tree of Life," which is this *Sefer HaZohar,* and they will leave exile in mercy, and *"God alone*

will lead them, and they will have no foreign god" (*Devarim* 32:12).[10] (*Zohar* 124b)

That's what it is all about, isn't it? We want to leave exile, but we want to end it mercifully, without any further suffering and devastation. That, the *Zohar* seems to say, depends upon us, and the depth to which we understand the events of history, and the Heavenly messages they represent.

---

[10] This is what Moshe *Rabbeinu* had told Rabbi Shimon bar Yochai, the author of the *Zohar*.

Deeper & Deeper Yet

five

THE TALMUD SPEAKS of an incident during which the son of a great rabbi of that time, Rebi Yehoshua ben Levi, almost died. However, just before complete death his soul returned, and when he awoke and regained consciousness, he found his father sitting by his bedside.

Sensing that his son had been on the brink of death, he asked him what he saw while there. The son answered:

> *"An upside down world. What is up over here is down over there, and the opposite is true as well."*

"No, my son," Rebi Yehoshua ben Levi corrected him. "In truth, you saw the *real* world. It is *this* world that is upside down." (*Pesachim* 50a)

It is a powerful story with an equally powerful lesson, but it begs the question: How can something be so obvious to one person and yet so unclear to another?

That enemies do not see eye-to-eye is precisely why they are enemies. But fathers and sons, friends and allies—how can *they* see so differently, especially with respect to something as fundamental as good and evil in everyday life, with respect to what is truly important and what is trivial in this world?

The trouble with reality is that it is multi-layered. If there were only one level to reality, then life could be as black-and-white as we'd like to believe it is. But then again, if it were, wouldn't life cease to challenge us? A person would learn something once and that would be it; nothing more to learn here anymore.

However, fortunately that is not the way life is. Life is about learning something, and then learning it better, and then learning it *deeper*. A wise person knows that few things in life are what they seem to be on the surface, whereas the fool simply assumes that what he sees is all there is to know.

Unfortunately, enough such people from the latter group can bring the world to the brink of destruction. I say to the brink *only* because God has stepped in countless times to save us from ourselves. Left alone, this group would have destroyed the world many times over.

However, if we were to bring enough of the former group together, we could usher in *Yemos HaMoshiach*, may it happen quickly (and painlessly) in our time. It is this group that is capable of consistently seeing truth, and directing life accordingly.

The average person does not realize how much he is affected by what he knows—or doesn't know—and how it colors the way he perceives what goes on around him. He just assumes that what he perceives is *all* there is to perceive. Until, of course, he finds out otherwise, often too late, and often at the cost of many lives.

Let's say, for example, a person was raised as a secular Jew. Assimilated, he didn't care about the concept of God and didn't even know what Torah is, let alone live by it. If you told him, "Next year at this time you will be an Orthodox Jew," he would probably think that you were crazy and possibly be offended by what he would consider an insult to his intelligence.

Yet, let's also say that, like so many before him, he travels to Israel and UNEXPECTEDLY[1] ends up in a class about Judaism. And, let's say that the teacher

------

[1] That is, *Hashgochah Pratis* leads him there.

happens to be good enough and the material he presents interesting enough to inspire this assimilated Jew to come back to a second class, a third one, and a fourth one, etc. It happens much of the time in similar situations.

Perhaps, as far as he is concerned, he is not learning about Judaism, just about something that interests him. After all, very little that he is learning resembles anything he had previously been taught about Judaism. It is certainly not the Judaism he had grown up with, as many often point out along their path to *teshuvah*.

In the course of the learning, issues come up that previously interested or concerned him but which he never knew or dreamed were addressed by Torah. Interest piqued, he decides to stay and investigate this new brand of Judaism a little further, only to find himself committed to a Torah way of life exactly one year later. What changed?

What happened was that the "assimilated Jew" unexpectedly tapped into a wealth of knowledge he came to PERCEIVE to be crucial for a meaningful life, and was open enough to admit it to himself. This led to further investigation, which in the Torah world begins with philosophy and leads to, eventually, the performance of *mitzvos*.

Typically, the *Ba'al Teshuvah*, the technical term for a Jew who returns to the path of Torah (whether he was previously observant or not), begins with *Chumash* (Five Books of Moses). Soon after, he begins to learn Mishnah, the essence of the Oral Law and Torah observance, and *Halachah*,[2] which explains the implementation of the *mitzvos* in everyday life.

As his knowledge base widens, he discovers a desire to know God and to feel His Presence. It is a new sensation, something he had NEVER felt until that time. It is something that he had never known he could ever feel or care about, like all Jews who are distant emotionally from Torah and *mitzvos*.

After entering the world of Talmud, most of the doubts and discomforts with which he had begun have faded, answered through the Talmud or with its help. It took time to adjust to a lifestyle so radically different from the one to which he had been accustomed, but the wisdom to which he has since been exposed is far greater than anything he ever previously knew. He even discovers answers for questions he had yet to formulate.

Years later, he has become proficient at learning and has even earned his *smichah*—rabbinical ordination. Perhaps he can still recall images from his "previous life," but he no longer feels any emotional attachment to them. The transformation of another secular

---

[2] From the Hebrew word that means "walk," since Jewish law is the "path" a Jew must walk towards fulfillment.

Jew to a Torah way of life has been completed.

Such is the power of knowledge; such is the power of *Torah* knowledge. The true *Ba'al Teshuvah* does not change his way of life; he changes his intellectual understanding about life, its goals, and its opportunities. The rest, such as the change of lifestyle, naturally takes care of itself. What we think and believe guides our actions, and all the external changes, hopefully, are just natural expressions of all our inner changes.

Unfortunately, many stop at this point in their Torah development. Until this level, the learning was both vertical and horizontal. Vertical learning is when we add new ideas to our knowledge base, while horizontal learning is when we delve deeper into ideas with which we have already become familiar. Both are crucial for fulfillment, though we don't always do them at the same time.

However, once many *Ba'alei Teshuvah* settle into *Yiddishkeit*, they often sacrifice depth for breadth. Torah is so vast, and there is so much to learn that one can easily spend their entire life learning only on the "surface" of Torah, and find fulfillment doing so. Many have, and many do.

Fulfillment *yes*, the Big Picture, *no*.

What is the *Big Picture?*

It is the vision to which Rebi Yehoshua ben Levi alluded when his son recovered from the throes of death. More precisely, it is the vision *beyond* the vision, the deeper layers of Torah understanding. It is the knowledge that God gave to the Jewish people to allow them to rise above the everyday reality, first by understanding the inner workings of Creation, and then by working with them to fulfill their mandate.

Not many Jews go this far with their Torah learning these days, even many of the very learned. However, if we do, we would better understand the undercurrents of history, past and present, which will provide a more accurate context for the events of daily life. On this level of Torah consciousness, only *true* good can be seen as good, and true evil as evil; there is never any mistaking the two in the realm of *Sod*.

And, to achieve this, all one has to do is enter *Pardes*, as the next chapter will discuss.

SIX

DID YOU EVER wonder where the English word "Paradise" came from? In a biblical sense, the concept of Paradise is usually a reference to the original paradise, the Garden of Eden, which had been nothing other than a *"pardes."*

In English, the word means "orchard," which is what the original garden was. Thus, it would not be too big a stretch of one's imagination to see the word *"pardes"* as the source of the English word "paradise," especially since so many English words have biblical origins.

However, based upon an account in the Talmud, we learn that a *pardes* refers to more than a physical garden, and therefore, that the Garden of Eden was far more than simply a physical paradise.

The story is as follows:

> The rabbis taught: Four entered *Pardes:* Ben Az-
> zai, Ben Zoma, Acher, and Rebi Akiva. Rebi Akiva
> told them, "When you arrive at the Stones of
> Pure Marble, don't say, 'Water, water,' because it
> says, *'He who speaks falsehood will not be estab-
> lished before My eyes'* (*Tehillim* 101:7)." Ben Az-
> zai gazed at the Divine Presence and died, and
> with respect to him it says, *"Difficult in the eyes
> of God is the death of His pious ones."* (*Tehillim*
> 116:15). Ben Zoma gazed and went mad; to him
> the following verse may be applied: *"Have you
> found honey? Eat as much as is sufficient for
> you, so that you do not consume too much and
> have to vomit it"* (*Mishlei* 25:16). Acher "cut off
> his plantings" (i.e., he became a heretic). [Only]
> Rebi Akiva entered in peace and departed in
> peace. (*Chagigah* 14b)

At this point, we don't know much about the
pardes these four rabbis visited other than the fact
that only one survived the experience. However, the
Talmud commentary of *Tosfos* explains:

> That is, by way of a Name—they didn't actually
> go "up," rather it appeared to them as if they

went up. (*Tosfos*, q.v. *Nicbnas l'Pardes*)

In other words, *Tosfos* is explaining, these four rabbis meditated on one of the Names of God to intellectually transcend levels of Torah consciousness, to which the word "*Pardes*" alludes. Indeed, though the word itself means "orchard," the four letters are in fact the first letters of four other words: *Pshat, Remez, Drush,* and *Sod*.

As it is well known, Torah can be learned on four distinct levels: *Pshat, Remez, Drush,* and *Sod* (literally: Simple, Hint, Exegetical, and Mystery). This means that a Torah concept, like reality itself, has many levels of meaning, from the simple to the most sublime.

In fact, these four levels of learning also correspond to four areas of Torah learning: *Mikrah* (*Chumash*), Mishnah, Talmud, and Kabbalah respectively. Thus, "entering" *Pardes* is also a process of going from one area of Torah learning to a higher one, from *Pshat,* to *Remez,* to *Drush,* and finally to *Sod*.

Another way of looking at these four levels is as layers, concentric spheres that overlap each other like layers of an onion. *Pshat* represents the most outer, obvious layer, while *Sod* represents the most hidden, inner, and *essential* layer. In fact, *Sod,* being the most inner layer, is said to be clothed by *Drush,* which is clothed by *Remez,* all of which are clothed by the most outer layer, *Pshat*.

For example, the first word of the Torah is "*Bereishis*," which is generally translated as, "*in the beginning*." This is the simplest explanation of this word, and therefore it is the *Pshat* of this word.

However, as *Rashi* points out, the form of the word is actually grammatically incorrect. If one wants to say, "in the beginning," he should instead write, "*b'rishonah*." Now, since the Torah is perfect and was dictated by God to Moshe *Rabbeinu* letter-by-letter, the fact that "*Bereishis*" was not spelled grammatically correct, *Rashi* explains, HINTS to a deeper level of meaning.

Thus, *Rashi* explains, the word "*bereishis*" can actually be read as two words: "*reishis*" with the letter *Bais*. Thus, on the level of *Remez*, the first word of the Torah no longer only means "in the beginning," but can also translate as, "*for reishis*," which, as *Rashi* proves, is an allusion to Torah and the Jewish people. On this level of explanation, the *verse* would read:

For the sake of Torah and the Jewish people, God made Heaven and Earth.

However, beyond this, there is nothing more unusual about the word to suggest to the *physical* eye even deeper layers of understanding. To go beyond the level of *Pshat* and *Remez* is a matter for the *mind's* eye,[1] and usually a function of a known tradition passed down from generation to generation. This is the level of *Drush*.

Continuing with our example, we know from the Torah that the world was created in six days, and that all the matter for the six days of Creation came into being, at least in potential, the moment God said, "*Bereishis*." And, not just for the six days of Creation, but for the six millennia that followed as well, like a script that is written and completed in advance of the play. The question is, is there an allusion to this idea in the word itself?

The answer emerges when the word "*bereishis*" is once again divided into two parts, but this time between the first three and the last three letters of the word. This yields two smaller word: "*bara*" and "*shis*," which mean, "He created six," "*shis*" being the Aramaic form of the word, "*shaish*," which means "six."[2]

Thus, exegetically, the first word of the Torah reveals a very important philosophical fact: when God made the world *ex nihilo* on Day One of Creation, He created the potential for *anything* and *everything* that would *ever* exist in Creation at that first moment.

---

[1] That is, the knowledge of other principles force a deeper understanding of a concept to maintain intellectual consistency.

[2] *Sha'ar HaPesukim* 1:1; *Succah* 49a; This is not the only instance of Aramaic in the Torah (*Megillah* 9a).

Nothing in history, therefore, can ever be considered random.

What about the level of *Sod*? What Kabbalistic teaching emerges from the word *bereishis* that reveals to us a secret about Creation?

On this level of explanation, the word *bereishis* is once again divided into two as on the level of *Drush*. However, this time the word *"shis"* alludes not only to the six days of Creation and the subsequent six millennia, but also to the six *sefiros* of *Chesed* through *Yesod*, spiritual emanations into which God encoded the script for 6000 years of history:

> This is why so much time must transpire from the time of Creation until the time of the *tikun* (i.e., *Moshiach's* coming): all the forces of *Gevuros* are rooted in the six *sefiros*—*Chesed, Gevurah, Tifferes, Netzach, Hod, Yesod*—which are the six days of Creation, and also the six thousand years of history that the world will exist. And within them (the six *sefiros*) are the roots of all that will happen from the six days of Creation until the Final Rectification. (*Drushei Olam Ha-Tohu* 2:151b)

The significance of this information may not be obvious to one unfamiliar with the *Sefiros*. However, for our purposes, it is enough to know that within one word, there are four layers of meaning, each one true, but each one more specific and revealing than the previous one.[3] And, even though one level may allude to a deeper level of explanation than itself, that deeper level is only revealed once the "clothing" of the previous level has been "removed," which is necessary if one wants to get to the essence of an idea.

However, the intellectual gap between each of the four levels is not equidistant. Indeed, the difference in depth of understanding between *Pshat* and *Remez—Mikrah* and Mishnah—is less than the difference between *Remez* and *Drush*— Mishnah and Talmud. This is easily evident once one has experienced all three areas of Torah learning.

Furthermore, the difference between the level of *Drush* and *Sod* is far greater than the difference in levels of understanding between *Remez* and *Drush*, even though *Sod* is one of four levels of learning. In fact, the first three letters of *Pardes* spell the word *"pered,"* which means "separation," because they are separate from the realm of Kabbalah.

Thus, the four rabbis who entered *Par-des* entered an intellectual paradise, so-to-speak, which is what made it so dangerous. For, to go beyond one's intellectual capability is to damage oneself, perhaps

---

[3] The *Zohar* actually provides 70 different interpretations of the word *"Bereishis."*

even fatally. This was, in essence, what God told Moshe *Rabbeinu* on top of *Har Sinai:*

> *No one can see My face because no man can see Me and live!* (*Shemos* 33:20)

As the Kabbalists explain, "face" here refers to a more direct revelation of God, which is the end result of successfully entering *Pardes* to the greatest extent possible.

According to the *Zohar*, the reason why Rebi Akiva and his colleagues had entered *Pardes* was to change the course of history. It had been just after the Romans had destroyed the Second Temple, and Jewish blood flowed through the streets from massacre after massacre. Rebi Akiva had planned to lead his group into the deepest and most hidden levels of *Sod*, in order to rectify the sin of Adam *HaRishon*, and bring history into *Yemos HaMoshiach*.

However, as the Talmud recounts, he barely escaped with his life, let alone rectify the sin of Adam *HaRishon*. Along the way, he lost three important and distinguished colleagues, one to death, one to insanity, and one became the quintessential heretic. Who is qualified to even enter *Pardes* as these rabbis did, if they themselves could not survive the intellectual journey?

Fortunately, even the realm of *Sod* is multi-layered, and the lowest of levels allows a much safer access, and crucial information for constructing the "Big Picture" of Jewish history and Torah thought. It is said that Rebi Akiva hid the "keys" for penetrating further than this level of *Sod* until *Moshiach's* time, though he left enough doors open to provide crucial insights for future generations of Jews.

A perfect example of this idea is the story of Iyov, or Job. The story of Iyov is the quintessential example of an age-old philosophical issue, that being *why do bad things happen to good people*. It is a question, according to the Talmud, that even Moshe *Rabbeinu* himself asked God while on *Har Sinai* receiving the Torah.[4]

Seemingly, Iyov had been a thoroughly righteous person who had done little wrong to warrant the personal destruction he experienced. Yet, prompted by God Himself, the *Satan*—the "Accusing Angel"— brought upon Iyov tremendous personal hardship, causing him to lose his wealth, his family, and even his own personal health.

The rest of the story is about Iyov coming to terms with his personal tragedy. First he, and then his friends, tried to find a *rational* explanation for his misfortune. With the exception of Elihu, they could find none, and therefore they concluded that Iyov could

---

[4] *Brochos* 7a.

not have been as righteous as they had previously thought. For, they assumed, God does not punish and allow suffering for no reason.

However, Iyov rejected their deduction, knowing full well that he had done everything in his power to be loyal to God. And, after his friends took leave of him and God Himself paid Iyov a visit, he took the opportunity to question God about what had befallen him.

However, rather than sympathize with Iyov, God criticized him sharply for even questioning His judgment. Instead, he asked Iyov:

> *"Who is this who disgraces [My judgment, which is made with] secret wisdom, with words [which he speaks] without knowledge [of the secret wisdom]?*[5]*... Where were you when I founded the earth? Tell [Me] if you have knowledge to understand its foundation?" (Iyov 38:1-4)*

From there, God took Iyov on an intellectual tour of the universe, showing him the tremendous wisdom with which He made Creation, and maintains it. And, in spite of the fact that God did not provide Iyov with a precise answer for his own personal tragedy, it seemed to have sufficed for Iyov, whose

---

[5] Based upon the *Ramban's* interpretation.

only response was:

> *"Behold, I am worthless, so how can I answer You? I place my hand on my mouth. I have spoke once, and I won't respond [again]. A second time, I will not [complain] anymore."* (*Iyov* 40:4-5)

Humbled by the awesomeness of the Divine wisdom, Iyov felt ashamed that he ever doubted the workings of his Creator. He came to realize from God's response that, as smart as man may be, his vision of reality is still incredibly limited, and therefore he is never capable of fully comprehending Divine judgment, if at all.

However, though Iyov himself may not have been aware of the cause of his suffering, apparently the Talmud was:

> Rav Chiya bar Avva said in the name of Simai: Three were involved in that advice [to enslave and oppress the Jewish people], and they were Bilaam, Iyov, and Yisro. Bilaam advised to kill them, Iyov remained silent and was punished with suffering, and Yisro fled and merited descendants who sat in the "office of hewn stone" (i.e., the chamber in which the *Sanhedrin* officiated). (*Sanhedrin* 106a)

It is so simple that you don't have to even resort to *Sod* to figure it out. Iyov had remained silent while standing before Pharaoh, and failed to cast the deciding vote in favor of freeing the Jewish people. And, since, as the Talmud teaches:

All the traits of The Holy One, Blessed is He, are [based upon the principle of] measure-for-measure... (*Sanhedrin* 90a)

measure-for-measure, for having remained silent in Pharaoh's court and allowing, at least indirectly, the suffering of the Jewish nation in Egypt, Iyov himself was punished with tremendous suffering.

Thus, even on the level of *Drush* there is an answer for why bad things happen to "good" people, at least with respect to the story of Iyov. Anyone who ignores the Talmud and simply reads the Book of Iyov enters the story in the middle, so-to-speak, and not at the beginning, and hence, *of course* questions are going to arise.

However, even though *in this case* the perplexing question is answered through the Talmud, in truth, it is still *Sod* that provides the *key* pieces of the puzzle that truly reveal the justice in what occurred to the righteous Iyov. It also explains why the *Satan* plays such a major role in the story, many years after Iyov has left the court of Pharaoh for his own home.

It took 116 years,[6] but eventually the end of the Egyptian exile came, and the Jewish people left Egypt en masse in the year 2448/1313 BCE. Nevertheless, as the Torah writes, Pharaoh regretted his decision to free the slave nation and pursued them with his best soldiers, and trapped them at the shores of the Red Sea.

However, God divided the waters and allowed the descendants of Avraham to flee to safety once again. The sea splitting also drew the Egyptian army into the sea after them, after which God returned the waters and drowned every last Egyptian (except for Pharaoh himself) who entered the sea. Awestruck and extremely grateful, the Jewish people sang praise to God, reciting the following *verse*:

> *Your right hand, God, is glorious in power; Your right hand smashes into pieces the enemy (Aleph-Vav-Yud-Bais). (Shemos* 15:6)

On the levels of *Pshat, Remez,* and *Drush,* there is nothing unusual about these words to suggest a deeper meaning. However, the *Arizal* points out, the letters of the word "enemy" are, in fact, the same letters as that of "Iyov" (*Aleph-Yud-Vav-Bais*), and this is

---

[6] The slavery did not begin until the year 2332/1429 BCE, after the last of Yosef's brothers, Levi, died in 2331 (*Seder Olam* 3).

not by coincidence, for it was Iyov who provided the means for the Jewish nation's escape across the sea.

How is that? The answer to that question comes from knowing what took place by the sea, just before it finally split and provided the fleeing Jewish people with dry land on which to tread. For, as the Jewish people stood in the water up to their necks and in a grave state of danger, it was then that the Prosecuting Angel—the *Satan*—hurled his accusations against the Jewish people before God.[7]

> "Master of the Universe," he argued, "did not the Jews worship idols in Egypt as well? Why do they deserve miracles?" (*Yalkut Shimoni* 1:234)

The truth was, as the Midrash points out, he had a good point. Indeed, the Jewish people, because of their previous deeds, warranted Divine punishment, and should have been left to drown right there in the sea. However, there was a problem, and that was that God had promised Avraham *Avinu* hundreds of years earlier:

> *On that day, God made a covenant with*

---

[7] Tradition teaches that it is during times of danger that the Satan prosecutes, in order to prevent miracles from happening to save us.

Avram, saying, "To your descendants I have given this land..." (Bereishis 15:18)

And, as the Talmud points out:

Every promise of good that comes from the mouth of The Holy One, Blessed is He, even if conditional, is never retracted. (*Brochos* 7a)

This, of course, created a dilemma. On one hand, there was the promise made to Avraham *Avinu* to eventually bring his descendants to *Eretz Yisroel*. However, the last of those descendants were neck-deep in a raging sea, with the Egyptian army ready to pounce on them from the other direction, while the Prosecuting Angel hovered above, removing all possibility of a miraculous salvation. What to do?

It is at this point that the Book of Iyov begins, reveals the *Arizal*:

> *God said to the Prosecuting Angel, "From where do you come?"*
> *And the Prosecuting Angel answered God, "From searching the earth and from traveling in it [looking for people's sins]."*
> *And God said, "Have you noticed My servant Iyov, that there is none like him on earth? [He is] a perfect and upright man who fears God*

and turns away from evil." (Iyov 1:7-8)

The Talmud has an expression: Do not open your mouth to the *Satan* (*Kesuvos* 8b), and the story of Iyov is the reason why. For, any type of bragging is a direct invitation to the *Satan* to come and investigate the merits and demerits of the one being praised, and if the investigation finds fault in the object of conceit, judgment can be swift and costly, perhaps even fatal.

Thus, speaking so highly of Iyov in the face of the Satan, God was, in effect, prompting an investigation into the merits and demerits of Iyov, and it is THIS that resulted in the supreme test he underwent. The only question is, since God knows this, *why did He do it?*

The answer is, to pull the *Satan* away from the Jewish people, in order to end his prosecution of them.[8] This way, God could perform the necessary miracle to save the Jewish people, and fulfill the promise to Avraham *Avinu*. In other words, after failing to be the vehicle of redemption from the Egyptians 116 years earlier when he had the chance to, Iyov was the vehicle for their redemption from the Egyptians—

---

[8] This is similar to the idea of blowing the Shofar on Rosh Hashanah to "confuse" the Satan and save ourselves from his prosecutions (*Rosh Hashanah* 16b; *Zohar* 1:114b; *Pesikta Rabosi* 41).

measure-for-PERFECT-measure—at the Red Sea.

However, the story of Iyov is not complete yet; *Sod* has more to say about the source of his suffering:

> Terach, Avraham's father, reincarnated into and was rectified by Iyov. (*Sha'ar HaGilgulim*, Chapter 36)

The truth is, this is really what Elihu told Iyov when he said:

> *[Consequently, God] has redeemed his soul from passing into Gehinom, and his living soul will see the light [of the World-to-Come, when the time comes for him to die]. (Iyov 33:28)*

> God in His kindness created the concept of *gilgulim*—reincarnations—in order that no soul should be expelled from the World-to-Come. (*Ramban, Rabbeinu Bachya*)

Yes, Elihu told Iyov, you are righteous in THIS life. However, what about in your previous lives, all of which make up the totality of your being. Is it not possible that you are rectifying today something that was wrong from the past, before you were even born into this reincarnation? Indeed, explains the *Arizal*, the concept of "the reward for a *mitzvah* is a *mitzvah*, and the reward for a sin is a sin" actually spans lifetimes.[9]

Thus, as is the case in most situations,[10] when *Sod* is infused into the levels of *Pshat, Remez,* and *Drush* of the story of Iyov, the perplexing questions become anything but that, falling away altogether. Having said this, we can now return to our discussion about the End-of-Days.

Perhaps calculating the precise time of *Moshiach's* arrival is risky business, but narrowing that time down to a specific period of time is crucial for appreciating the opportunities of history, and its present momentum. The following does precisely this:

> The [ninth *sefirah* called] *Yesod* [which is the cosmic script for the sixth millennium] divided into two "kings" (that is, into two independent *sefiros* prior to the first day of Creation, as part of the creation process, called) "*Yesod*" and "*Atarah*" (crown). The *Atarah* is relevant to *Malchus* (the tenth and final *sefirah*—and which means "kingdom"), since it is her crown, which is why it is called "*Atarah*."[11] Therefore, the

---

[9] *Sha'ar HaGilgulim,* Introduction 38.

[10] Including the well-known but disturbing discussion between God and Moshe *Rabbeinu,* which includes the gruesome death of Rebi Akiva (*Menachos* 29b).

[11] That is, in the system of *Sefiros,* the *Atarah* sits directly above the *sefirah* of *Malchus,* like a crown sits on a head.

Yesod and the *Atarah* [prior to Creation] became two; however, after the *tikun* (i.e., Creation), the *Yesod* and the *Atarah* became one in
order to join together *Zehr Anpin* and the *Nukvah* forever.[12] This is the *sod* of *Yemos HaMoshiach* being at the *end* of the sixth millennium, the
time when the *Atarah* governs and gives off light
for *Yemos HaMoshiach*; *Yesod* itself governs the
time of exile until *Yemos HaMoshiach*. Since the
Atarah is rooted in an independent "king" and
the *Yesod* divided into two, the sixth millennium,
which corresponds to *Yesod*, divides into two.
During the time which corresponds to the *Yesod*
there will still be destruction and exile. However,
the time that corresponds to the *Atarah* will be
Yemos HaMoshiach. (*Hakdamos uSha'arim*, p.
172)

Kabbalistic terminology aside, the basic point is
simple. The *Leshem* is explaining that, unlike the previous five *sefiros* of *Chesed* through *Hod* that governed the first five millennia of history, *Yesod*, which
governs the sixth millennium, has two distinct parts.
And, because *Yesod* has two distinct parts to it, the six

---

[12] The former term refers to a unit comprised of the six *sefiros*
from *Chesed* through *Yesod*, and the latter term refers to the
Malchus itself.

millennium must, by definition, have two distinct parts: exile and redemption, as in the FINAL redemption.

Thus, *Moshiach* MUST come before the end of the sixth millennium; it's an immutable mathematical reality encoded into the *Sefiros*. All one has to know is the exact proportion of *Atarah* to *Yesod*, and he can calculate the precise arrival date of *Moshiach*. Regarding this proportion, the *Leshem* added:

> [It is also a long period of time.] The entire period of time is referred to as *"keitz d'b'ittah"* (*end of in its time*), and this is the simple reading of the verse, *"I, God, will hasten it (achishenah) in its time (b'ittah)"* (*Yeshayahu* 60:22). The verse is promising that the entire period of *"b'ittah"* will not pass, rather that the time of redemption will be hastened, and that "early" will also be "in its time"; thus both terms will be fulfilled . . . It will not be delayed for the entire period of *b'ittah*, God forbid, but rather it will be hastened. (*Hakdamos u'Sha'arim*, 211)

In other words, as the Talmud has revealed,[13] there are two possible arrival dates for *Moshiach*: *achishenah* and *b'ittah*, two terms borrowed from the

---

[13] *Sanhedrin* 98a.

prophet's own words:

> *"I, God, will hasten it in its time—b'it-tah."*
> (*Yeshayahu* 60:22)

Thus, *"achishenah"* alludes to an earlier, and therefore NON-FIXED date for the arrival of *Moshiach*, making possible what the *Rambam* teaches in the twelfth principle of faith:

> I believe with complete faith in the coming of *Moshiach*. And though he may tarry, I know he can come any day. (*Thirteen Principles of Faith*)

And, because it is an *early* date, it is also one that is based upon the merits of the Jewish People. If the Jewish People prepare the world for *Moshiach's* arrival in advance of the last possible time, then *Moshiach* will come earlier. If the world is ready for the Final Redemption, why wait?

However, the second term *"b'ittah"* refers to a *final* arrival time for *Moshiach*, a fixed IMMUTABLE moment in history built into the master plan of Creation long before this physical world even existed. And THAT time, according to the *Leshem*, is the precise moment during the sixth millennium that the first phase of *Yesod* gives way to the second phase of *Yesod*, the *Atarah*.

Hence, it really is quite mathematical. The first phase of the *Yesod* represents a *specific* quantity of the entire *sefirah* of *Yesod*, and therefore of the sixth millennium. It is an *exact* fraction, and thus, if one could calculate that fraction, one could convert it into a precise date for *Moshiach's* arrival, even to the minute. It is to this amount that the *GR"A*—the Vilna Gaon—alluded when he wrote:

> Know that each day of Creation alludes to a thousand years of our existence, and every little detail that occurred during these days will have its corresponding event happen at the proportionate time during its millennium. According to this, you may recognize the [time of the] Final Redemption, if it comes at its appointed time, in case, God forbid, Israel is unworthy . . . (*Sifra D'Tzniusa*, Chapter Five)

Has anyone ever successfully made the calculation? Apparently, some have. Will we ever be able to make such a calculation. Apparently, yes:

> It is not yet God's will that the date of *Moshiach's* arrival be revealed to man, but when the date draws near, even children will be able to make the calculation and it will be revealed to all. (*Zohar, Bereishis* 118a)

This is presumably because the events of the time will make it impossible *not* to know just how close *Moshiach's* arrival time is. However, until such time—which may not be as far away as we think given current events and historical tides—let's deal with what we *DO* know.

It is presently the year 5763. We are, therefore, 76.3 percent through the sixth millennium, making the proportion of the first phase of *Yesod*, so far, just more than three-quarters long, and the *Atarah*, 23.7 percent long. That's roughly a 3:1 ratio.

On the other hand, if we accept that *Techiyas HaMeisim* is to begin, as the *Zohar* seems to indicate, no later than in the year 5790/2030 BCE, then the first stage of *Yesod* cannot be longer than 79 percent of the entire *sefirah* of *Yesod*, and the *Atarah*, no less than 21 percent. According to this, some time over the next 27 years the transition from the first part of *Yesod* to the *Atarah* must occur.

Maybe it is 26.5 years away, one could argue. Perhaps. However, additional pieces of information may reduce that figure as well, for, according to the *Leshem*, *Yemos HaMoshiach* will not be a momentary phase of history, but last for a period of time:

At the beginning of *Yemos HaMoshiach*, there will be a combination of nature and miracle working together at one time, as we saw at the time of the leaving of Egypt. Then, also, at the beginning of the redemption, there were great miracles, yet, the Jewish People still were quite physical and material; the *zuhama* was not removed from them until the giving of Torah . . . So, even though God dealt with them on the level of great miracles, still their lives were completely governed by nature. (*Sha'arei Leshem*, p. 488)

This is corroborated by the following *Midrash* from Rabbi Noson Shapiro:

There is a tradition that, at the time of the arrival of *Moshiach*, wonderful things will happen for Jews everywhere. On the actual day that they arrive from the Diaspora...the walls of *Yerushalayim* will be replaced. It will also be the day of the re-building of the Temple, which will be built from exquisite stones and gems. Once the dead are resurrected, they will become transformed and will have very lofty natures. However, the same type of transformation will occur for the... Jews who remained alive [in *Eretz Yisroel*], and their bodies will be like that of Adam *HaRishon* before his sin, and like Moshe *Rabbeinu's*. They will become so spiritual that they will be able to fly like eagles, which will astound the redeemed exiles. Upon witnessing this, the "Diaspora Jews" will become upset, and they will complain to *Moshiach*, "Are we not Jews like them? Why do they merit to fly and live in an elevated spiritual state, and not us?" However, *Moshiach* will answer them, "It is quite well known that God works measure-for-measure. Those who lived in the Diaspora and made efforts and sacrifices to elevate themselves by moving to the Holy Land merited purity of soul. They were not so concerned about their finances and health. They traveled over vast lands and crossed seas, not paying attention to the possibilities of drowning, being robbed along the way, or being taken captive by some strange foreign ruler. Being that they placed priority of their spirit over materialism and physicality, they merit, measure-for-measure, to be elevated to this lofty spiritual plane. On the other hand, *you* who also had opportunities to go up to Israel, but remained hesitant and reluctant, enamored instead with your materialistic status, making materialism a higher priority than spiritual growth, therefore, *measure-for-measure*, remain physical." (*Tuv HaAretz, Praise Of Those Living In Eretz Yisroel When Moshiach Arrives*)

Furthermore, according to tradition, the transition itself will have its own transition:

> One *verse* says, *"Who magnifies—magdil—the victories of His king"* (*Tehillim* 18:51), and one *verse* says, *"He is a tower —migdol—of His king's salvations"* (II *Shmuel* 22:51). Rebi Yudan says: It is because the redemption for this people will not come all at once, but will progress over time. What does "magnify" —*magdil*— mean? It will become increasingly larger—*misgadeles*—and continue. For this reason, the redemption is compared to dawn, as it says, *"Then your light will burst out like the dawn"* (*Yeshayahu* 58:8). (*Midrash Shochar Tov, Mizmor 19*)

However, asking how long the period called "*Yemos HaMoshiach*" will be is tantamount to revealing the date of his arrival.[14] Regardless, we are no longer dealing with hundreds of years as many people believe, and many who have succeeded materialistically would like to continue to believe. However, as Rabbi Moshe Feinstein, *zt"l*, warned decades ago:

Despite the conditions of hardship and dire

---

[14] All one would have to do is count backwards from the year 5790 to know when the period is supposed to begin.

poverty in Europe, European Jewry produced great Torah-luminaries, unmatched by the American Jewish community. In analyzing the cause for this, we recognize as one of the major factors [American] parental pressure that children attend college to secure themselves a good living. This prevents them from concentrating on Torah study. In addition, it has become an accepted philosophy in Jewish circles that it is the goal of life to attain as many luxuries and as much enjoyment as possible, but in a *"kosher"* manner, of course. Although someone raised in America is not required to content himself with the frugal standard of living which was the norm in Europe, nevertheless, a Jew must not think that it is correct to seek the fulfillment of all *possible* desires. Aspirations to buy an elegant car or a luxuriously furnished house with the most modern gadgets generate the need for money . . . It is clear then that we should not seek to yet raise our standard of living. If we only resist the *yetzer hara* that demands all attainable luxuries, we will be able to spend less time on business and find more time for Torah-study. (*HaGaon* R' Moshe Feinstein; Jewish Observer, June 1975)

Based upon all of this, all events that occur at this stage of history have great significance. Whether it is the inauguration of a new leader, or a terrorist attack somewhere in the world, it means more today than it would have years ago. The politics in Israel and yes, their resultant detrimental effect on the religious community, are more profound at this precarious period of time. And, rapidly rising anti-Semitism has a *raison d'être*, though so many Jews may resist seeing it, or are even oblivious to it.

The Talmud warned:

> Rav said, "All the dates of redemption have already passed, and now it depends upon repentance and good deeds." Shmuel said, "It is enough that the mourner remains in mourning!" This is like an earlier disagreement: Rebi Eliezer said, "If Israel will repent then they will be redeemed, and if they will not, then they will not [be redeemed]." Rebi Yehoshua said to him, "If they do not repent they will not be redeemed?! Rather, The Holy One, Blessed is He, will cause to rise a king who will make decrees as difficult as Haman's were and Israel will repent and return to the right path." (*Sanhedrin* 97b)

Look *closely*. Look *deeply*, and perhaps even *deeper* yet. It is there that The Holy One, Blessed is He, left behind the clearest clues, the biggest picture, to help those who are willing to help Him bring history to its ultimate conclusion. The more we know, the better prepared we will be.

*The Centrality
of Eretz Yisroel*

seven

ONE OF THE surprising things about *Shas*[1] is how much attention it pays to the topic of *Eretz Yisroel*. The Talmud is based upon the *Mishnah*, which for all intents and purposes is the section of Torah referred to as the "Oral Law."

It is the Oral Law that defines the 613 *Mitzvos* (which are only referred to in the "Written Law"—the five books of the Torah), providing the crucial details necessary to properly implement the *mitzvos* in daily life. The issue of *Eretz Yisroel*, at least in the minds of

---

[1] The Hebrew letters are *Shin-Samech*, and stand for *"shishah sidrei"*—the "Six Orders" of the Talmud: *Zerayim* (Seeds), *Moed* (Holidays), *Nashim* (Women), *Nezikin* (Damages), *Kodashim* (Holy Things), and *Taharos* (Purity).

many Jews today, is at most a *hashkofic* matter, not a *halachic* one.[2]

True, the Torah writes:

> God told Moshe, "Speak to the entire congrega-
> tion of the Children of Israel and tell them, 'Be
> holy, for I, your God, am holy.'" (Vayikra
> 19:1-2)

Seemingly, this "commandment" means that a Jew is *obligated* to pursue holiness to the best of his ability. It means that a Jew has to pursue closeness with God, Who is exceedingly holy, thereby necessitating that *we* be holy as well. If so, it follows, if *Eretz Yisroel* is the holiest place in the world, should not the Jew also pursue a life in *Eretz Yisroel?*

Theoretically, yes, as the Talmud—recorded by great rabbis who lived in Babylonia at the time—states in no uncertain terms:

> The rabbis taught: A person should rather live in
> *Eretz Yisroel*, even in a city whose majority of
> inhabitants are gentile, than outside the Land,
> even if the majority of the city's inhabitants are

---

[2] The former term means "philosophical," and the latter term means "legal."

Jewish. All those who dwell in *Eretz Yisroel* are like those with a God, and all those who dwell outside the Land are like those *without* a God. (*Kesuvos* 110b)

However, *practically*-speaking, not necessarily, as *Tosfos* points out in the following:

We are not accustomed at this time [to live in *Eretz Yisroel*] because of the danger along the way, and *Rabbeinu Chaim* says that at this time there is no *mitzvah* to live in *Eretz Yisroel* because there are many *mitzvos* and punishments related to the land, and we are not careful enough in performing them. (*Tosfos, Kesuvos* 110b, q.v. *"He says, 'Let's go up' "*)

To this very day, many cite this *Rabbeinu Chaim* when questioned about their lack of desire and motivation to make *aliyah* and live in the Holy Land.

The only thing is, regarding the first part of *Tosfos*, it was written back in the thirteenth century and wouldn't apply to today. In the days of *Rabbeinu Chaim*, travel to and from *Eretz Yisroel* was an obvious danger: if the means of travel didn't kill a person, the bandits and anti-Semites he could meet along the way would.

However, *today*, travel to and from *Eretz Yisroel*

is a common occurrence that people rarely think about twice; few people worry about the kinds of problems the travelers of *Tosfos'* time were certain to experience along the way. Thus, perhaps for this reason, reluctant Jews focus more on the second aspect, that is, *Rabbeinu Chaim's* concern about life in the Holy Land: *mitzvos* dependent upon the land.

As it is well-known, there are some *mitzvos* that apply only to *Eretz Yisroel*, such as the *mitzvah* to tithe produce of the Land, or to allow it to remain fallow once every seven years.[3] True, such *mitzvos* are only rabbinical during times that there is no Temple, but we still take them quite seriously even today.

Furthermore, *Eretz Yisroel* is a holy land, the holiest in the world. Being so, it has less tolerance for those who sin, and therefore it is more likely to be a cause of Divine wrath for disobedience. It is the only land capable of "spitting out" its inhabitants if they do not live in accordance with the Torah; it is safer to sin in *Chutz L'Aretz*, or so the argument goes.

However, regarding this concern of *Rabbeinu Chaim*, it seems that later rabbis either disagreed with it or no longer felt that it was a reason to avoid making *aliyah* to *Eretz Yisroel*. One of those rabbis was the *Gaon* from Vilna himself—the *GR"A*. On the contrary, explains the *GR"A*, it is *specifically* those *mitzvos* re-

---

3 Of a *Shmittah* cycle.

lated to the land of *Eretz Yisroel* that we must perform to pave the way for *Moshiach's* arrival:

> The following are the circumstances and manners of Redemption…Eradicating the impure spirit from *Eretz Yisroel* by planting the Holy Land. The three groups of exiles depend on this, according to the *Gaon*, especially the commandments concerning leaving the poor man the gleanings of the crop, the forgotten sheaf, and the corners of the field. How much should be planted and to what extent? The land should be planted until it is no longer desolate, until the holy land bears its fruit. The goal is to drive out the spirit of impurity from the land, to purify the holiness of the "Revealed God" from its *klipah*, etc. The holiness of the Revealed God rests upon the fruits of the Holy Land. This is the *sod* of the reason for the *mitzvah*, *"When you come to the land you shall plant…"* (*Vayikra* 19:23). According to the Midrash, you should not occupy yourself with anything except planting, and this was the main part of the mission of the Vilna Gaon… (*Kol HaTor,* Chapter 7)

Furthermore, the *GR"A* revealed to his students that:

The war against Amalek is in every generation. The war against Amalek is against three types of foes: a) Amalek of the heart, that is, the evil inclination and vices; b) the spirit of Amalek, the general one, the *Satan* who destroys—the adversary of Israel. This is *Sama"el* and his hosts. His main power is in the gates of Jerusalem, when its lands are desolate; c) the material Amalek, that comprises Eisav and Yishmael and the *Erev Rav* (Mixed Multitude). As explained by the *Gaon*: we are commanded to inherit it [the Land, if need be] by force. The strength and rulership of Amalek's spirit is in the gates of Jerusalem, as mentioned above, but only when there is destruction and desolation near the gates and in the unwalled areas of Jerusalem. As long as the spirit of impurity rules there, the feet of the cypress tree cannot stand there. This delays the connection between the Jerusalem of below and the Jerusalem of above, that is the connection between the *Shechinah* and *"Knesses Yisroel"* on which the entire Redemption depends. The war against the desolation is waged not only by setting up tents of Ya'akov and dwelling places of Israel in their respective places, but also by planting its land and fulfilling the commandments dependent on it. The war against the material Amalek always depends on the time and place, and necessitates counterattacking (lit., "returning the battle to the gate") with force, as in the days of Ezra and Nechemiah, and like the conquest during the days of Yehoshua. (Ibid.)

Hence, the words of the Talmud quoted above retain their impact, especially when the Talmud makes other statements such as this one:

Anyone who walks four *amos*[4] in *Eretz Yisroel* is assured a portion in the World-to-Come. (*Kesuvos* 111a)

In other words, the Land of Israel is so holy and so precious to God that He even rewards those who just *walk* in it. Therefore, while walking to perform a *mitzvah* in *Eretz Yisroel,* one actually fulfills two *mitzvos* simultaneously: the *mitzvah* itself, and that of walking in *Eretz Yisroel* in the process.

Is there a better way to maximize one's portion in the World-to-Come? Is that not what we are here to do in the first place?

Elsewhere, the Talmud says:

A person who sees himself in a dream unclothed

---

[4] A distance of 6 to 8 feet.

in Babylonia is without sin (*Rashi*: Because outside the land there is no merit, only sin, and one
who stands without clothing there is like one
lacking those sins); in *Eretz Yisroel*, he is without
mitzvos (*Rashi*: Because there are many *mitzvos*
there, and to be naked is a sign of being without
mitzvos). (*Brochos* 57a)

According to this interpretation, though sins
count *everywhere* in the world, *mitzvos* only count in
Eretz Yisroel. Fortunately for those who live in *Chutz
L'Aretz*, this is not the prevalent opinion: *mitzvos* DO
count when performed there. However, this does not
mean that there is not an aspect of this idea that is not
true on some level. After all, the Talmud does say:

Three inherit the World-to-Come, one of whom
is he who lives in *Eretz Yisroel*. (*Pesachim* 113a)

and:

One who lives in *Eretz Yisroel* lives without
transgression. (*Kesuvos* 111a)

—implying that just living in *Eretz Yisroel* has a certain
power of atonement, like Yom Kippur itself. This is a
crucial element for earning the World-to-Come, espe-

cially with a limited amount of time in *Gehinom*.[5]

Indeed, *Eretz Yisroel* is in good company:

> Three wonderful gifts were given by The Holy
> One, Blessed is He, to the Jewish people, and all
> of them were given through hardship. They are
> Torah, *Eretz Yisroel*, and The World-to-Come.
> (*Brochos* 5a)

Contemplating this statement alone should
make it clear what *Eretz Yisroel* is about. It is also highly significant that *Eretz Yisroel* is mentioned second,
after Torah, assuming that the Talmud has listed the
three in ascending order of importance.

True, a Jew can survive without *Eretz Yisroel*, but
not without Torah. However, the Talmud implies, it is
Eretz Yisroel that allows a Jew to best fulfill the Torah
and to achieve personal completion; together they
lead a person to the World-to-Come. Therefore, if one
is prepared to "suffer" to learn Torah and to earn the
World-to-Come, why does he expect life in *Eretz Yisroel* to be a "piece of cake," and get frustrated when it
is not?

The following makes the relationship of Torah,
Eretz Yisroel, and the World-to-Come even clearer:

---

[5] Purgatory.

Ten measures of wisdom fell to the world, nine of which fell on *Eretz Yisroel*, and one on the rest of the world. (*Kiddushin* 49b)

The air of *Eretz Yisroel* makes a person wise. (*Bava Basra* 158b)

Hey, aren't we about wisdom? Of course we are. Then what is holding us back from returning to the Holy Land in order to embrace a way of life for which we are supposed to still be yearning, especially when the Talmud concludes elsewhere:

Eretz Yisroel lacks nothing. (*Brochos* 36b)

Eretz Yisroel was created before the rest of the world. (*Ta'anis* 10a)

God personally waters *Eretz Yisroel*; the rest of the nations receive sustenance through a messenger. (*Ta'anis* 10a)

Eretz Yisroel receives rain, but the rest of the world just receives the residual. (*Ta'anis* 10a)

The rabbis taught: If a person is married to a woman for ten years and she does not give birth for him, he should divorce her and give her a *kesuvah*, because maybe he doesn't merit to build a family through her. Even though there is no proof for this, there is an allusion to it: *"Sarai, the wife of Avram took Hagar the Egyptian, her handmaid, after Avram dwelled in the land of Canaan for ten years, and gave her to Avram..."* (*Bereishis* 16:3). We learn from here that his stay outside of Israel did not count [in the ten years]. (*Rashi*: He was with Hagar, which means he did not marry her before he came to *Eretz Yisroel*, though there were many years spent in Padan Aram [childless]. This teaches you that the time outside the Land did not count for him; perhaps the transgression of [living] outside the land caused her to be barren). (*Yevamos* 64a)

Why is *Eretz Yisroel* compared to a deer? Just like the skin of a deer does not contain its flesh, neither does *Eretz Yisroel* contain its fruit[6]...so too is *Eretz Yisroel* the fastest to ripen its fruits... (*Kesuvos* 112a)

---

[6] The skin on a deer is extremely tight, giving the impression it cannot contain its own flesh. However, in the end, it stretches according to the needs of the deer. Likewise, tiny *Eretz Yisroel* can miraculously expand to accommodate all of the needs of its people.

Just like the skin of a deer does not contain its flesh, neither does *Eretz Yisroel* contain its flesh when they live on her.[7] (*Gittin* 57a)

Eretz Yisroel is higher than all other lands. (*Kiddushin* 69b)

How could something so central to the Jewish people become so secondary?

---

[7] See the previous note.

*A Matter of
Above & Beyond*

eight

WITHOUT DOUBT, LITTLE gets the back of a Jew up more than the idea of making *aliyah* when there is no desire to do so. In fact, *aliyah* is such a controversial topic today, particularly in many Orthodox circles, that one would think that we were living back in the time of the Ottoman Empire, when the land remained uninhabitable! It is as if there isn't an already thriving Jewish population there, and as if Torah institutions had yet to be built when in fact, in some communities, they exist in one form or another on every block!

But that's okay, people think, since there is no *halachah* today compelling Jews to return home after 2000 years in exile.

That is correct—there is no *halachah* today to make *aliyah*. *BUT*, when it comes to Torah observance, there are really *two* aspects: *halachah* and something else that many may know little about—*inyan*. And, the surprising thing is that, even though an *inyan* may seem less important, less obligatory than *halachah*, it turns out that it may actually be the best expression of all a Jew has become.

Halachah is Jewish law, and therefore obligatory when applicable. Whether the origin of the *halachah* is an actual Torah *mitzvah* or a rabbinical ordinance, it is binding upon all Jews to whomever and whenever it applies. The only difference between the two sources of *halachah*, for the most part, is whether or not one can be lenient in extenuating circumstances. In any case, a Torah authority should be consulted before taking such a liberty.

However, what is an *inyan*, and is it binding?

Literally, *"inyan"* means "matter," as in the concept of a topic; it is not binding because it is not *halachic* in nature. But if not, then what is its *raison d'être*; don't Jews already struggle enough with what *is* obligatory?

The answer to this question is the following, and the *Ramban's* explanation of what it means:

God told Moshe, "Speak to the entire congregation of the Children of Israel and tell them, 'Be

holy, for I, your God, am holy.' " (Vayikra
19:1-2)

In my opinion, this "separation" is not from forbidden relationships, as [*Rashi*] says, but it is the
kind of separation mentioned throughout Torah
when it comes to being elevated. For, the Torah
warned us regarding forbidden relationships and
forbidden foods, but it also permitted spousal
intimacy and [kosher] meat and wine. Thus, a
person with strong physical desires could be-
have "promiscuously" with his own wife, or with
many women [to whom he is also married], and
eat [kosher] meat and drink wine in a disgusting
manner, since the Torah has not forbidden this
[outright]. Nevertheless, [if he acted in this
manner] he would be a *"menuval b'reshus Ha-
Torah"*—"disgusting with that which the Torah
permits." Therefore, after the Torah specified
what is certainly forbidden, it returned to tell us
that we should exercise restraint with that which
is permissible. (*Ramban, Vayikra* 19:2)

Now, if you look in the *Minyan HaMitzvos* at the
beginning of *Parashas Kedoshim* where it lists all the
mitzvos found in the upcoming *parsha*, you will see
that the first *mitzvah* recorded is the one to fear one's

parents. According to the *Minyan HaMitzvos*, and all commentators concur, the first *mitzvah* of the *parsha* is not to "*be holy*" mentioned in the first verse, but the *mitzvah* to fear one's mother and father taught in the next verse.

Does this mean that there is no *mitzvah* to be holy? How can that be? Hasn't the Torah already said:

> *Moshe went up to God, and God called to him from out of the mountain, "Tell the house of Ya'akov, and the Children of Israel: 'You have seen what I did to Egypt, and how I bore you on eagles' wings, and brought you to Myself. If you will obey My voice and keep My covenant, then you will be unique to Me above all the nations, for all the earth is Mine. You will be a kingdom of priests to Me, a HOLY nation.'"* (Shemos 19:3-6)

Thus, holiness is what we, the Jewish people, *are all about.* Indeed, holiness is what Creation as a whole is all about:

> At that time [Resurrection of the Dead, 5790-6000], a great change will occur to the entire world, even to those still in existence from this world, though they remain quite physical. For, at the present time, the world consists of three cat-

egories: impure, pure, and holy, and even the "pure" of today is still quite profane, lacking holiness. However, at that time, everything will be on the level of pure and HOLY. (*Sha'arei Leshem*, p. 491)

In fact, the two words that the *Kohen Gadol* wore on the *Tzitz*, the special gold plate that he wore on his forehead, "*Kodesh L'Hashem*"—Holy to God— was not just a directive to him and those who served in the Temple. It was a reminder for the *entire* Jewish people of our purpose here on earth, to be a holy nation and to elevate the rest of Creation to this high spiritual status.

Thus, being holy is the goal of all that the Jew sets out to accomplish, which is why *Parashas Kedoshim* comes in the middle of *Sefer Vayikra*, and not at the beginning or the end of it. It is as if the Torah is saying, "Now that I have taught you all the *technical* laws regarding your daily lifestyle as a nation of God, we can finally begin to discuss the *INYAN* of *kedushah*, of holiness."

Thus, it says:

Rebi Pinchas ben Yair said: Watchfulness leads to zealousness, zealousness leads to cleanliness, cleanliness leads to purity, purity leads to separation, separation leads to HOLINESS , holiness leads to humility, humility leads to fear of sin, fear of sin leads to piety, piety leads to holy spirit, and holy spirit leads to resurrection of the dead, which will come through Eliyahu *HaNavi*, may he come and redeem us quickly in our time. (*Sotah* 49b)

Just like *Parashas Kedoshim* itself, the *mitzvah* to be holy is the level one reaches by keeping all technical *mitzvos* possible. And, it is an indispensable rung on the spiritual ladder to climbing to higher heights, the end goal of the Jewish people.

To lose sight of this, says the *Ramban*, is to take the Torah's silence as permission to abuse that which is permissible, yet holy. There is no such permission, the *Ramban* is saying on behalf of the Torah, for a holy nation such as the Jewish people. Rather, the Torah's silence is actually saying: Through the laws, about which you have little or no choice, I have brought you to the door of holiness. At this stage, it is your own personal will and desire that must carry you across that threshold.

It is for *this* that we were created. It is for *this* that God redeemed us from Egypt. It is for *this* that we will be evaluated at the end of days.

Therefore, what is an *inyan*? It is an idea or act that expresses that which the Jewish people are all about. An *inyan* represents that for which a Jew is supposed to strive *through* keeping Torah and *mitzvos*, that little extra that shows God whether or not we got His message.

As such, an *inyan cannot* be obligatory, any more than the *"nedavos haleiv"*—"gifts of the heart" used in the construction of the *Mishkan*—could be. How do you command someone to give of their heart; how do you command someone to love another if they don't already?

You don't. In fact, this is the explanation given for the *Rambam's halachah* regarding the *mitzvah* to love God. The *Rambam* wrote:

> What is the path to loving Him and fearing Him? When a person contemplates His works and His awesome and mighty creations, and sees in them incomparable and endless wisdom, IM-MEDIATELY he will love, praise, glorify, and greatly desire to know his Great Name, as Dovid wrote, *"My soul thirsts for God, the Living Almighty"* (*Tehillim* 42:3). (*Yad, Hilchos Yesodei HaTorah,* 2:1)

What is the "path" to loving Him? Who was talking about paths? Why doesn't the *Rambam* just say, "There is a *mitzvah* to love God, so do it, or transgress a very central tenet of Torah!"?

Because, the *Rambam* understood, emotions

cannot be commanded, but are the end result of our perceptions and experiences. Therefore, the *Rambam* is instructing, if you want to love God, create the proper perceptions and experiences that result in such an emotional response. And, to do THAT, says the *Rambam*, is simply a matter of appreciating the world that envelopes and supports you.

An *inyan* works in very much the same way. It facilitates the proper perception and experience to love and come close to God, and it is also the result of them. And, as the opening midrash revealed, though there is no *mitzvah* to make *aliyah* at this time of history, prior to *Moshiach's* arrival, there is a very important *inyan* to do so.

Furthermore, though *inyanim* rarely push off *halachah* (if at all), it seems that sometimes they can mitigate a *halachah*, as in the case of Purim being in the second month of Adar in a leap year. There, the *inyan* of having the redemption of Purim close to the redemption of Pesach pushes off the *halachah* of doing a *mitzvah* the first chance we can.[1]

---

[1] *Megillah* 6b. There is a law that states one should not pass up an opportunity to do a *mitzvah* (*Yoma* 33a). If so, then Purim should be in the first month of Adar in a leap year, because that is the first possible time to celebrate it. However, in order to keep Purim and Pesach close to one another, which is only an *inyan*, we pass up the opportunity of the first Adar and instead wait to celebrate Purim in the second month of Adar.

Thus, though there may not be a *halachic* obligation to move to *Eretz Yisroel* at this time in history, there is certainly an *inyan* to do so, and at the very least, to *yearn* to do so. However, before one sits back and says, *"Great, there is ONLY an inyan to be there!"* he has to first realize that this may be the most compelling reason of all to make *aliyah* at this time, and why there is such a great reward for those who did, before it became obligatory in *Moshiach's* time.

In fact, there is another very powerful concept that comes to play in this discussion, though it only makes what appears to be a "guest appearance" in the Torah. Indeed, it is so central to all that the Jew is about that we even developed an expression around it: *zrizim makdimin l'mitzvos*—zealots are quick to perform *mitzvos*.[2]

The idea is not complicated to understand. People who love and value what they do are anxious to perform it *well* every chance they can. And, when the reason for that love is the source of the opportunity itself—which in the case of *mitzvos* is God Himself— then the willingness to perform the act and the care with which it is executed is a display of that very love. Thus, the expression really means: Jews who love God perform *mitzvos* zealously.

---

[2] *Pesachim* 4a.

There is a special name for zealousness in Judaism, and that is *"kena'os."* Not coincidentally, it is derived from the same word for "jealousy" (*kinah*), because Jewish zealousness is none other than jealousy on behalf of God, as we learn from the Torah:

> *God told Moshe, "Pinchas, the son of Elazar, the son of Aharon the Kohen, stopped My anger towards the Children of Israel because he was zealous on My behalf, which prevented Me from destroying them because of jealousy."* (*Bamidbar* 25:10-11)

Essentially, a *"kanoy"* is someone whose very being is intertwined with the truth of Torah and love of God, to the point that any violation of Torah is also a violation of his or her self. As such, it is impossible for the *kanoy* to stand back and watch the violation occur, but rather, he will take action—either peaceful or aggressive—to rectify the situation.

In other words, one who performs *mitzvos* with zeal is as much of a *kanoy* as one who avenges God and Torah, as Pinchas did when he killed Zimri.[3] In fact, they are usually one and the same person, meaning that a true *kanoy* is *always* a *kanoy,* as in the case

---

[3] *Bamidbar* 25:8.

of Rebi Chanina ben Teradyon.[4]

However, the tricky and extremely dangerous part of being a *kanoy* is making sure that the feelings of jealousy are truly on behalf of God, and not mixed together with a personal agenda. Personal motives sour the performance of a *mitzvah*, and transform acts of zealousness into far less noble acts, as happened to Shimon and Levi, the sons of Ya'akov *Avinu*.

To avenge the violation of their sister Dinah by the prince of the city of Shechem, Shechem ben Chamor, they zealously slaughtered all the men who lived there.[5] Yet their father, Ya'akov *Avinu*, on his death bed criticized their act, saying:

> *"Shimon and Levi are brothers. Their means of acquisition are instruments of violence. My spirit will not enter into their councils; my honor, do not be identified in their assemblies. For in their anger they murdered men, and of their own free will they maimed an ox." (Bereishis*

---

[4] *Avodah Zarah* 18a. The Talmud subtly makes this point by showing that Rebi Chanina ben Teradyon was someone who gave up his own money for the poor with as much zeal as he taught Torah in public at the risk of death. The small, hidden act of giving *tzedakah* he did not have to give—without any regret—revealed that his self-sacrifice for Torah in public was altruistically motivated.

[5] *Bereishis* 34:25.

49:5-7)

Furthermore, it is only pure *kena'os* that invokes true Heavenly help, allowing the *kanoy* to achieve superhuman feats to succeed at being zealous. Thus Mordechai, the hero of the Purim story, was able to topple the once-powerful Haman—in only 70 days! Regarding Pinchas himself, the Talmud states:

> Rebi Yochanan said: Six miracles happened for Pinchas . . . (*Sanhedrin* 82b)

—without which he could *never* have succeeded until the glorious end to receive the reward that he did:

> *"Therefore," [God said], "I give [Pinchas] My covenant of peace. The covenant of the priesthood will be his and his descendants forever because he was zealous for his God, and atoned for the Children of Israel." (Bamidbar 25:12-13)*

And, not only does true *kena'os* draw down special help from God, but it even results in opportunities that might otherwise have been reserved for greater people:

> *Moshe told the judges of the Jewish people. . ."*

(*Bamidbar* 25:5)

The tribe of Shimon went to Zimri ben Salu and
said to him, "They are judging cases of life and
death and you sit in silence?" What did he do?
He gathered together 24,000 Jews and went to
Cozbi (the Midianite princess sent by Balak and
Bilaam to tempt Moshe). He said to her, "Heed
me!" She answered him, "I am the daughter of a
king, and my father told me to heed none other
than the greatest among them!" He (another
person there) told her, "He [Zimri] is also the
prince of a tribe, and not only that, but he is
greater than [Moshe], because he (i.e., his ancestor Shimon) was born second [to Leah, his
mother], whereas he [i.e., Moshe's ancestor,
Levi] was born third [to Leah]!" Immediately, he
grabbed her braid and brought her to Moshe
and said to him, "Son of Amram! Is this one forbidden or permitted? And, if you answer forbidden, then who permitted [Tzipporah, your Midianite wife] to you?!" [At that moment,] the law
was hidden from [Moshe], and they all (Moshe
and the judges with him) began to cry, as it says,
*"They were crying at the opening of the Ap-
pointed Tent"* (*Bamidbar* 25:6). And [then] it
says, *"Pinchas ben Elazar saw"* (Ibid. 7). But
what did he *see*? He saw what was happening

and remembered the law, and said to [Moshe], "Brother of the father of my father! Did you not teach us when you descended from *Har Sinai* that if a Jew is intimate with a gentile, the zealots should kill him?" He answered him, "The one who reads the letter should deliver it." (*Sanhedrin* 82a)

In other words, Moshe *Rabbeinu* understood—from the fact that he forgot the law and that Pinchas remembered it—that Heaven had singled out Pinchas to carry out the *mitzvah* of *kena'os*, though he himself was perfectly prepared to do so. Indeed, the rabbis write:

"They were crying at the opening of the Appointed Tent" (*Bamidbar* 25:6): their hands became weakened at that moment. To what can this be compared? To the daughter of a king who was adorned in preparation to go to the *chupah*, and instead is unfaithful with another. Do not her father and relatives become distraught? Likewise, at the end of the 40 years, as the Jewish people camped by the Jordan river ready to cross over into *Eretz Yisroel* . . . they went ahead and acted promiscuously, weakening Moshe and the righteous people with him. *They cried?!* Did he [Moshe] not stand up against 600,000 [at the

time of the golden calf], as it says, *"He took the calf which they had made"* (*Shemos* 32:20), [and yet you say that] his hands were weakened?! Rather, [Moshe was *made* to forget the law] in order for Pinchas to take that which he deserved. (*Bamidbar Rabbah* 20:24)[6]

This concept is also used to explain why it was the daughters of Tzelofchad who were the vehicle, later on in the same *parsha*, to teach an important law regarding the inheritance of *Eretz Yisroel*.[7] Moshe could have easily taught the same law as he did all the other *mitzvos*. However, because of their intense love of *Eretz Yisroel*, a function of their own *kena'os*, the daughters of Tzelofchad merited to be recorded in the Torah *forever* as the cause of the new law.

In each case, it was not that the *Gadol HaDor* lacked or lost the merit to provide the direction at the critical moment in time. Rather, it was that someone else lesser than they merited to be the instrument of God at that moment in time. In fact, in each case, Moshe *Rabbeinu* had to be "held back" by Heaven in order to "make room" for the *kanoy* to do his "thing."

And, as we quoted previously, Dovid *HaMelech*

---

[6] *Rashi* (*Bamidbar* 25:6) quotes the same idea in the name of the *Tanchuma*.

[7] *Bamidbar* 27:1; *Bava Basra* 119a; *Sanhedrin* 8a.

indicated and the Vilna Gaon emphasized that re-demption, at least in the initial stages, is a function of *kena'os*.

The beginning of anything, whether great or small, connected with the footsteps of the *Moshiach* must be by the designated people, that is, the emissaries, messengers of above at the beginning of the Redemption, which will occur with designated deeds, and designated events. The two together will hasten the desig-nated times, that is, the times of the ends of the footstep levels (of which there are 999 in the *sefirah Yesod*) that are connected with the be-ginning of the Redemption when the awakening comes from below. The emissaries will begin the deeds and hasten the designated times. This is attested to in the verse *"You will arise and show Tzion mercy, for [there will come] the time to favor her, for the appointed time will have come"* (*Tehillim* 102:14). When will this be? *"For your servants have cherished her stones, and favor her dust." Then the other nations will fear the name of God, and all the kings of the earth Your glory. For God will have built Tzion, He will have appeared in His glory"* (Ibid. 15-17)…What can hasten the "designated time"? It is possible to hasten deeds, but how can one hasten a designated time that was determined beforehand?...Whenever a deed is done as a result of the "awakening" from below, Divine judgment is aided by the [Divine] lovingkindness...and thus, every designated time will be cut in half. This is what is meant by, *"for [there will come] the time"*: it means we will not have to go as far as the designated time [for the Final Redemption], but rather the time will come to us after *"your servants have cherished her stones and favor her dust"*...Similarly, the Midrash on the verse, *"a redeemer will come to Tzion"* (*Yeshayahu* 59:20) denotes that the coming of the Redeemer depends upon the rebuilding of Zion. (*Kol HaTor,* Chapter 4:3)

It is an act of *kena'os* to cherish the stones of *Eretz Yisroel* and "favor her dust" when such love and longing is born out of the fact that *Eretz Yisroel* matters so much to God—*at any time in history*. How much more so is this the case at a time that *Eretz Yisroel* and the Jews living there are the scorn of the world!

And, the truth is, as long as anticipating the redemption and making *aliyah* remain only an *inyan*, only zealots will follow through with doing so. Or, they will live with the disappointment of being prevented from doing so because of more pressing Torah obligations. But never are they satisfied with the present state of exile, no matter how comfortable it has become for the Jewish people.

However, once the *Gedolei HaDor* make the decision that the time has come for Jews to return to the land of our Forefathers, it will cease to be an *inyan* to make aliyah and instead become a *halachah*. True, there is always room for a little *kena'os* even when it comes to the obvious details of performing a *mitzvah*, that is, as long as free-will exists. However, the opportunity is greatly lessened for God-fearing and rabbi-obeying Jews once the *halachah* is finalized from the top.

Thus, when it comes to being a *kanoy*, either you are one already, *or you are not.* The level to which one is a zealot is the sum total of all one's Torah learning and fear of God; it emerges from the person and it is not something that can be taught. Indeed, it is the only law for which there is no section in the *Shulchan Aruch*. Indeed, the Talmud says that if someone comes to a *rav* asking if he can perform the act of *kena'os*, he is to be told no. It is as if to say, "If you have to ask permission to be a *kanoy*, then you probably aren't one anyhow, and it is not *your* opportunity to sanctify the Name of God."

It is from those gray areas of history and from amidst the "silence" that *kanoyim* usually emerge, often to the surprise of all those around. What Dovid

HaMelech, a true *kanoy* himself who suffered much at the hands of others, wrote regarding himself:

> *The stone the builders despised became the cornerstone. (Tehillim* 118:22)

could be applied to countless worthy zealots throughout Jewish history. Indeed, the Jewish people's initial response to Pinchas' act was to kill him for murdering a prince of Israel!

Is that what is going on today with respect to the Jewish people? Are we misinterpreting the "silence" as confusion amongst the Torah giants of today and as a lack of leadership, God forbid. Or, are we misinterpreting it as a decision *not* to take redemption and *aliyah* seriously—although many *Gedolim* in *Eretz Yisroel* do promote the idea?

This is true of *Gedolim* in the past as well. For example, the *Chofetz Chaim* wrote:

> If we really want Eliyahu and *Moshiach* to come we must make the proper preparations for them. The situation may be compared to someone who invites several honored guests to his house for dinner, and when the people arrive, he begins taking dishes out of the cabinet and raw food from the refrigerator to prepare the meal. Such a person would certainly be consid-

ered a fool for leaving all the preparations to the very last minute, and furthermore the guests would be completely justified for feeling deeply insulted that their host did not take the trouble to make the minimal advance arrangements for their visit. We beseech God several times a day—hundreds of times a year—in our prayers to send us Eliyahu and the *Moshiach*, but in fact we do not go to the slightest trouble to make even the most minimal preparations for *Moshiach's* advent. When the Temple is rebuilt will we be prepared to offer the sacrifices called for by the Torah? Torah scholars occupy themselves with many varied sections of the Torah and the Talmud, but very few people study the laws of these sacrifices, although they make up a significant percentage of the volume of Torah literature. Some people would retort, "When the *Moshiach* comes, he will reveal all the secrets of the Torah, and he will teach us exactly what to do! Why waste time studying before he comes?" It is true that in the messianic era a great abundance of knowledge of the Divine will be showered upon mankind, as it says, *"I will pour out My spirit upon all flesh, and your sons and daughters will prophesy"* (*Yoel* 3:1). However, as it is said in the name of the Vilna Gaon, the effect that this outpouring of Divine wisdom will have upon any individual depends upon his own capabilities as cultivated and developed *before* the *Moshiach's* advent—those with less understanding will appreciate this Divine knowledge to a lesser extent and those with a greater preparation, and therefore a higher capacity for increased knowledge, will be able to get much more out of it. The Sages formulated a rule: "If someone tells you, 'I achieved (Torah knowledge) though I did not toil at it,' do not believe him" (*Megillah* 6b), and this applies to messianic times as well. (*Haggadah Berurah*, page 139)

Kena'os may not be for everyone, just as *Eretz Yisroel, for the time being*, is not the destination of choice for the masses of Jews in *Chutz L'Aretz*. However, for this *smaller* group of potential *kanoyim* among us, there is a small window of time to come and take what is rightfully theirs: a portion of *Eretz Yisroel* BEFORE *Moshiach* arrives.

Obstacles Along the Way

nine

WHICH CHILD DOES not grow up with the phrase, *"Cheaters never prosper"*? And, for which child is this lesson not a tough sale? After all, the world seems to be full of cheaters, many of whom seem to be doing quite well for themselves, at least in the meantime. Remember the upside-down world of the son of Rebi Yehoshua ben Levi?[1]

However, how many adults do not know that, in the long run, cheaters really do *not* prosper? Over the long term, good always seems to triumph over evil, though the latter has wreaked tremendous havoc on mankind trying to turn the table. And, when it comes

---

[1] Chapter Five.

right down to it, "A for effort" really is much better than the "A" the person received because he was born a genius.

Why is that? It is this way because, as the rabbis teach, the world was created based upon a very simple yet immutable principle:

> According to the effort is the reward. (*Pirkei Avos* 5:22)

Reward? Which reward?

It can't be talking about reward in this world, because the Talmud clearly states that such reward is not relevant to this period of history.[2] This world is more a function of a specific cause-and-effect relationship designed to allow Creation to reach its ultimate, Divinely-ordained goal,[3] either *because* of man's actions, or *in spite* of them. How else could concepts such *"Tzaddik v'rah lo,"* bad things that happen to good people, exist?[4]

Thus, the rabbis were speaking about the reward of the World-to-Come, which is based, we are told, completely on the effort we make to achieve it. True, we aren't supposed to perform *mitzvos* for that rea-

---

[2] *Kiddushin* 39b.
[3] *Sha'arei Leshem*, page 62.
[4] *Brochos* 7a.

son, but rather, because we love God and Torah.[5] Nevertheless, it is the reward that helps us to understand how important our efforts are before our Creator.

Even still, this world is so distant from that final reality that we have to be told by the *Rambam* that the concept of true reward and punishment is a matter of faith:

> I believe with perfect faith that the Creator, Blessed is His Name, does good to those who observe the *mitzvos* and punishes those who transgress the *mitzvos*. (*13 Principles of Faith, #11*)[6]

That's the program. It has been the program at least since man was created and it will continue to be the basis of history until *Moshiach* comes, the *yetzer hara* is done away with,[7] and free-will ceases to exist and be an issue. And, until such time, life will continue

---

[5] *Pirkei Avos* 1:3.

[6] As the Talmud states, in this world we bless God for both the good and the bad (*Brochos* 54a), whereas in the Time-to-Come we will bless Him only for the good, once we are finally able to see how even the "bad" was for a good purpose.

[7] *Succah* 52a. In fact, the *gematria* of "*nachash*" (snake) and *Moshiach* are the same: 358, to indicate that *Moshiach* will be the one to rectify that which the original snake—the *yetzer hara*—caused to mankind (*Pri Tzaddik, Chukas* 16).

to be a challenge, difficult, and seemingly even impossible at times, making spiritual survival and true personal greatness a matter of *emunah*—faith—and of deep understanding of the way God runs His world—*Pardes*.

To make sure we understand this, the Talmud provided an important insight:

> Three wonderful gifts were given by The Holy One, Blessed is He, to the Jewish people, and all of them were given through hardship. They are Torah, *Eretz Yisroel*, and The World-to-Come. (*Brochos* 5a)

God is good, the best there is. The good that He gives, therefore and by definition, must be the very best good that can be given to and received by man.[8] The Talmud is telling us that this amounts to Torah, *Eretz Yisroel*, and the World-to-Come.

Now, one would expect that any gift from God would be extremely holy and the greatest example of good and righteousness man could ever perceive. Everything should go well with such gifts, and all that they touch should turn to gold, figuratively-speaking.

With respect to the World-to-Come, we can assume that is the case, and the Talmud makes this clear

---

[8] *Derech Hashem* 1:2:1.

as well.[9] However, when it comes to Torah, the Talmud states:

> Torah can be a potion for life or a potion for death. (*Yoma* 72b)

A gift from God a potion for death? How can that be?

And then, of course, there is *Eretz Yisroel*. From the outset of our history as a nation, we rejected this "wonderful gift," beginning with spies in Moshe *Rabbeinu's* time who stamped it "Return to Sender." And, 39 years later, after they died out because of that sin, the descendants from the tribes of Reuven, Gad, and Menashe gave up their portion of the Land to remain on the east side of the Jordan river.[10]

One would think that a gift from God would draw people to it like bees to honey. Yet on many occasions, *Eretz Yisroel* has had just the opposite effect on the Jewish people, and today is no different. Given the current reaction of many Jews to the concept of *aliyah* alone, one can't help but wonder if the *Arizal's* words are in effect already:

---

9 *Brochos* 34b.
10 *Bamidbar* 32:1.

In the future, Moshe himself will reincarnate and return in the last generation, as it says, *"you will lie with your fathers and rise up"* (*Devarim* 31:16). However, in the final generation, the *"Dor HaMidbar"*[11] will also reincarnate with the *Erev Rav*,[12] and this is what the *verse* also says, *"this people will rise up."* Hence, there is not a single generation in which Moshe *Rabbeinu* does not return *b'sod*, *"The sun rises and the sun sets"* (*Koheles* 1:5) and, *"One generation goes and another comes"* (*Koheles* 1:4), in order to rectify that generation. Thus, the Generation of the Desert along with the *Erev Rav* reincarnate in the final generation, *"like in the days of leaving Egypt"* (*Michah* 7:15). (*Sha'ar HaGilgulim*, Introduction 20)

But what's the problem? Did we not just say that we are rewarded in the World-to-Come for the efforts we make? Does this not mean that the greater the effort we make, the greater the reward will be for us then, ultimately what we want? Does not the challenge of *Eretz Yisroel* indicate its spiritual importance and represent a supreme *free-will* opportunity, like Torah itself, to maximize our spiritual perfection?

---

[11] Generation of the Desert.
[12] The Mixed Multitude.

Of course it does.

However, we are drowning in *Pshat*—the simplest perception of past and present events. Indeed, one of the most distracting developments in recent Jewish history from the main point of *Eretz Yisroel* to the Jew was the establishment of a *secular* Jewish state.

That *Eretz Yisroel*—or at least a portion of it—was "returned" to the Jewish people in the last century after being out of our hands for just over 2,000 years, was nothing short of a miracle and tremendous message from Heaven. After all, all that happens is a function of *Hashgochah Pratis* and a message to the Jewish people. However, the only question was, *what was the message?*

It could have been a Divine invitation to all Diaspora Jews to complete the process of *Kibbutz Golios*, the long-awaited process of ingathering the exiles to *Eretz Yisroel*. It certainly facilitated that process, though to a disappointing degree, since many Jews at the time and since then did not "hear" such an invitation to return home, for a variety of reasons.

For many secular Jews living abroad, *Eretz Yisroel* is only a partial homeland. With little, if any at all, belief that *Eretz Yisroel* is the God-given homeland of the Jewish people, why should they uproot themselves from existing lands of opportunity and comfort to drain swamps in a deserted land and build its infrastructure from the ground up? To have done so, from this perspective, would have verged on self-torture.

Not that they didn't feel a need for a Jewish homeland, or admire those who were prepared to build it. Therefore, many new funds were begun, and Jewish financial support from around the world began to flow in to the tiny new state, providing some crucial financial assistance for the new Israelis.

For the Religious Zionists, the creation of the new Jewish homeland represented nothing less than the advent of the Final Redemption. Regardless of the fact that the new government couldn't even manage to *overtly* insert God anywhere in their declaration of statehood,[13] the Jewish people were home after 2000 years of exile, seemingly a long-awaited fulfillment of ancient prophecies.

They knew then, as all Torah Jews believe, that the time will come when all Jews will once again recognize God and His Torah, and commit themselves to it. It's just a matter of time. Thus, an extremely secular state was still an important link between the Promised Land of the past, and the one, God willing, of the future. Thus, as far as *they* were concerned, that future had begun in 1948.

---

[13] The United States even prints it on their money.

For the *Charedi* community, the fact that *Eretz Yisroel* was to be governed by Jews with little or no concern for Torah, and even less respect for those who lived according to it, was certainly no cause for celebration. On the contrary, it even appeared to many that the creation of a secular state was a step *backwards,* after more than a century of building up the religious *yishuv* with great self-sacrifice.[14]

The seeds of mistrust had been sown long before the Secular Zionists had moved in. For hundreds of years, Torah Judaism had been fighting off assimilation and inter-marriage. Long and bitter exile, together with the *Haskalah* Movement,[15] had greatly depleted the ranks of Torah Jewry, with few, if any signs of improvement. Thus, the paranoia of the Torah leadership

---

[14] As early as the 1800s, students of the Vilna Gaon and Chassidic masters and their disciples began to settle in Tzfas, Tiberias, Hebron, and Jerusalem. They laid the foundation for what would be known as the *Yishuv HaYashan*. From that time onward, they built and enlarged Orthodox communities, which they populated and which became home to later waves of religious Jews emigrating from Russia and Eastern Europe.

[15] The movement began around 1763 with Moses Mendelssohn, who is considered to be the spiritual father of the famous motto of the nineteenth century *Haskalah*, or Jewish Enlightenment: "Be a cosmopolitan man in the street and a Jew in your home" (Triumph Of Survival, *Enlightenment, Reform, and Modernity*, p. 44).

was well justified and inevitable, and stemmed from a sincere love for God, Torah, and His people.

However, as Divine Providence would have it, the political and financial backing was in the hands of the secular Israeli world at the time, and by that time, so were the demographics. As a result, for the Torah Jews in *Eretz Yisroel*, it resulted in a type of siege-mentality, emphasizing the need for special protection from a government that overtly expressed its desire to secularize the ENTIRE Israeli population.

On the other hand, for the Torah Jews of the Diaspora, it meant the *geulah* had NOT come. Therefore, there was no need *yet* to seriously consider leaving the shores of America for the swamps and deserts of *Eretz Yisroel*. At least not yet, not as long as the goals of Torah, seemingly, could be better served in *Chutz L'Aretz* than *b'Aretz*. After all, historically, we can and have survived without a homeland for thousands of years now. However, we CANNOT and HAVE NOT survived without Torah.

In the meantime, post-Holocaust Jewry courageously and remarkably re-built itself on two fronts, in *Eretz Yisroel* and in the Diaspora. Well, *physically*, at least. For, as the tiny new state emerged as an independent power in the very large and openly hostile Middle-East, as world Jewry became a political force to be reckoned with in many countries where it was based, assimilation and inter-marriage became even more rampant, reaching crisis proportions.

And, as Israelis dug in to guarantee their continued presence in the Middle-East, Diaspora Jews became even more entrenched in their host countries as a result of financial success and political acceptance. On the contrary, Israel's constant need for cash and self-defense only seemed to underscore the importance of Jews remaining in *Chutz L'Aretz,* in order to generate tremendous amounts of capital and political support for the rapidly growing Jewish state.

Some 60 years later, the situation has changed little. Perhaps now, more than ever before, the state is fighting for survival. Thus, Diaspora Jews, for the most part, feel no obligation, not from within or from without, to shore up the Jewish population in *Eretz Yisroel.* Some TWO-THIRDS of the Jewish world still reject *Eretz Yisroel* as a valid place to live today.

Hence, there are many groups of Jews today that do not yearn to grace the soil of *Eretz Yisroel* with their permanent presence, for one reason or another. Thus, even though for 2,000 years Jews yearned to return to *Eretz Yisroel* but could not come, today, even though the door has been flung wide open and they *can* come, they no longer want to come. It's a strange twist of fate, *isn't it?* Rebi Yehoshua ben Levi was right: this world is *truly* upside down.

Too bad, because, according to the Vilna Gaon, the yearning for *Eretz Yisroel* is the final key to the Final Redemption:

> The purpose of redemption is the true redemption and sanctification of God's Name. According to the words of our prophets and the explanation of our teacher (*Vilna Gaon*), the goal of our work is the war against Armelius (the ministering angel of the *Erev Rav*), carried out through the ingathering of the exiles and settling of the Land for the sake of the true redemption and the sanctification of God's Name...These are the main components necessary for initiating the redemption from below: 1) ingathering of the exiles; 2) building of Jerusalem; 3) removal of impurity from the Land by planting the Holy Land and fulfilling the *mitzvos* dependent upon the Land; 4) true redemption resulting from the establishment of faithful people [in the gates of Jerusalem]; 5) sanctification of God's Name [through victory against Gog and Magog]; 6) revealing of the secrets of Torah; 7) rectification of the world...But, how can one bring closer the appointed times (*moadim*)...that were established at the beginning [of time]?...Every initiating act below which is from the left side of judgment is assisted by the trait of kindness from

the right...[In other words,] we don't need to reach the appointed time (*moed*), but rather, the *moed* will come to us—after "*Your servants have cherished her stones and favor her dust*" (*Tehillim* 102:14-15). (*Kol HaTor*, Chapter 4:1-3)[16]

As mentioned earlier, actually *making aliyah* at this stage of history is a *personal* event, dependent upon one's personal circumstances. Obviously other *mitzvos*, such as, for example, taking care of aging parents who cannot or will not make *aliyah* may prevent a person from moving to the Holy Land, for the time being.

However, what is *not* personal to the individual, but is, instead, incumbent upon the ENTIRE Jewish nation, is a *mitzvah* to *yearn* to live in *Eretz Yisroel*, for all the reasons stated throughout *Tanach*, the Talmud, and *Sifrei Kabbalah*. It is part and parcel of the obligation to yearn for redemption, to yearn for the days of "*Tzion*."

And, as the Talmud reveals, if a person TRULY wants to perform a *mitzvah* (as opposed to lip service only), but is prevented from doing so for reasons beyond his or her control, then Heaven considers the

---

[16] Regarding the oath to not ascend to *Eretz Yisroel* by force (*Kesuvos* 111a).

mitzvah to have been completed nevertheless.[17] We are only responsible for failure when our own negligence interferes with the performance of a *mitzvah*.

This is crucial to know, for it means that a person "detained" in *Chutz L'Aretz* can still have the status of being a *"B'nei Eretz Yisroel."* And this, as we have seen already, will make a big difference for him in the future in *Yemos HaMoshiach*[18] and on the Day of Judgment.[19]

Rabbi Yechezkel Levenstein, *zt"l*, was the famed *Mashgiach* of the Mir Yeshivah in Europe before the war, and the Mir of Jerusalem after the war, as well as the Ponovez Yeshivah in B'nei Brak. As mentioned in the Introduction, he said that such a yearning for redemption is part of an even greater *mitzvah, the all=important first of the Ten Commandments.*

Powerful words from a powerful Torah leader of the past—from *within* the midst of eastern European *"yeshivishe"* Jewry. And, if you think about it, logical words as well. In fact, like many situations throughout history, the present relationship of Jews to *Eretz Yisroel* does not make sense, and only exists because

---

[17] *Brochos* 6a.

[18] See the beginning of Chapter Eight.

[19] We can assume, though, the opposite for those who live in *Eretz Yisroel*, but who yearn to live in *Chutz L'Aretz* and would be there already if technical difficulties didn't stand in their way.

nothing has happened to change it. And, *mistakenly*, patience from Heaven has been taken to be tacit approval from Above.

Well, is it? How can we know? Without prophets to tell us what God is thinking, how can we be expected to understand a message we have never received?

Never received?

Never received? Does not opening the "envelope" in our hands constitute *"not receiving."*

Weren't we given the Torah on four levels—*Pshat, Remez, Drush,* and *Sod?* Do they not contain specific details to help us slice through the confusion of this upside-down world, and right it for ourselves? Look at how Moshe *Rabbeinu* described *Eretz Yisroel* to his father-in-law, Yisro:

> *Moshe said to Chovav, Moshe's father-in-law, the son of Reuel, the Midianite, "We are journeying to the place which God said He would give to us. Join us. You will benefit, for God has spoken good concerning Israel." (Bamidbar 10:29)*

He didn't refer to it as *Eretz Yisroel,* or even as Canaan. He called it "the place," another name for God Himself, as if to say to Yisro that going to *Eretz Yisroel* is tantamount to "going" to God Himself, so what could be better? No wonder God became so angry at the spies, and Moshe at Reuven, Gad, and

Menashe. And, it seems from history, the only way to break the pattern and rise above the obstacles along the journey there is by venturing through *Pardes* along the way.

Fooled As Well

ten

HOWEVER THERE IS more to the *Eretz Yisroel* issue than meets the average eye, whether we are dealing with the discouraging developments in the Holy Land, or the lack of inspiration to make *aliyah* from Torah leaders. And, in order to appreciate this idea, we have to go back in time to the days of the Jewish people in the desert, and the notorious Balak and Bilaam.

The *Shem M'Shmuel*[1] asks a question, one that all of us should ask when we reach *Parashas Balak*: Why did Balak and Bilaam think that they could ac-

---

[1] A series of books on the weekly *parsha* from the *Sochotchover* dynasty.

complish what Sichon and Og could not? Had they not learned from Amalek, Sichon, and Og, that attacking the Jewish people is self-destructive?

Furthermore, why did they even care? Balak had been the king of Moav,[2] a nation the Jewish people had not been permitted to attack.[3] Bilaam came from Midian, a nation to the south and far beyond the intended borders of *Eretz Yisroel*. Therefore, the question is, what drew them out of their safe havens to risk destruction at the hands of the approaching Jewish nation?

In his answer, the *Shem M'Shmuel* reveals a powerful insight into *Eretz Yisroel* and the Jewish people, one that has to be a best kept secret of all time:

> Their intention was based upon the following. If the Jewish people entered the land, then they would perform the *mitzvos* dependent upon the land, which would have the effect of purifying all physicality and sanctifying the ENTIRE earth...Then all bounty would become holy, and the nations of the world, who survive off a portion of this, would have to humble themselves to the side of holiness, or not prosper.

---

2 Jordan today.

3 *Devarim* 2:9.

This would force them to abandon their evil and detestable ways in order to become fitting to receive blessing from holiness. (*Shem M'Shmuel, Balak*, 5670)

This is something, *apparently*, Balak and Bilaam had not been prepared to do.

Therefore, unlike the nations of Canaan, which had fought the Jewish people as a matter of *physical* defense, Balak and Bilaam had fought against the Jewish people as a matter of *spiritual* survival, in order to allow evil to maintain its existence. However, had the ENTIRE Jewish nation entered *Eretz Yisroel* and settled the land,[4] quite *automatically*, the Final Redemption would have occurred, and the likes of Balak and Bilaam would have been no more—*forever*!

Thus, like Amalek who also had not been one of the nations of Canaan, and therefore not on the war agenda of the Jewish people, Balak and Bilaam uprooted themselves and went out of their way to confront and interfere with the approaching Jewish nation. And, as if to bring home the connection between these three enemies of the Jewish people, the *Zohar* reveals:

---

[4] According to the Vilna Gaon, this amounts to 600,000 male Jews above the age of 20 years, the number necessary to neutralize the *Sitra Achra* (*Kol HaTor*, 1:15:3)

What is the [spiritual] root of Amalek above? For, we see that the souls of Bilaam and Balak come from there. For this reason, [Amalek] is included in their names, in the "*Ayin-Mem*" of Bilaam (B*ais-Lamed-AYIN-MEM*) and the "*Lamed-Kuf*" of Balak (B*ais-LAMED-KUF*). (*Zohar, Ki Seitzei*, 281b)

Thus, the combination of Balak and Bilaam results in a reality of Amalek. However, when their names are combined, they actually yield two words: "*amalek*" and "*bavel*" (Babylonia)—the latter being the name of the country to which the Jewish people were first exiled, some 850 years after entering the Land under Yehoshua's leadership.

In other words, even though Balak and Bilaam died for their efforts—*a true Amalekian trait*[5]—they also succeeded in holding off the Final Redemption by causing part of the nation to reject its portion of *Eretz Yisroel*:

The descendants of Reuven and Gad had a lot

---

[5] *Rashi* explains the trait of Amalek: All the nations were afraid to war against Israel and this one came and led the way for others. It is like a boiling hot bath into which no living being could enter, until a wild person came and jumped into it. Although he scalded himself he made it cooler for others (*Rashi, Devarim* 25:18).

of cattle, and saw that the land of Ya'azer and Gilad was a good place for cattle. The descendants of Gad and Reuven approached Moshe, Elazar the kohen, and the princes of the congregation, and asked, "Ataros, Divon, Ya'azer, Nimrah, Cheshbon, El'aleh, Sevam, Nebo, and Beon, in the land which God struck before the Children of Israel is a land for cattle, and we have cattle. Therefore, if it is good for you, allow us to take it. Do not require us to cross the Jordan." (Bamidbar 32:1-5)

Is that all *Eretz Yisroel* meant to the tribes of Reuven, Gad and Menashe? *Yes*, and the Midrash has the following to say about them:

Likewise, you can take out the children of Gad and the children of Reuven, who were wealthy and had large flocks. They loved their property and dwelled in *Chutz L'Aretz*, and therefore were the first of the tribes to be exiled.[6] *(Bamidbar Rabbah 22:7)*

But *how?* How could people who lived such a holy existence, and witnessed such miracles as did the Jews of that time, become so materialistic and relin-

---

[6] To Assyria in 555 BCE.

quish their portion in holy *Eretz Yisroel?* The answer is: Balak and Bilaam, and the daughters of Midian.[7]

As the Torah reports, the daughters of Midian had been sent in, upon Bilaam's advice, to cause the Jewish people to stumble. Why them? Because, as a nation, Midian represented *"Klipas HaTa'avah"*[8]—the trait of intense materialistic desire. Thus, spiritually infected by this negative trait through the interaction with the women of Midian and their idol, Ba'al Peor, the emphasis of Reuven, Gad, and Menashe shifted to more materialistic matters.

Apparently, that's the way it has remained for thousands of years until this very day. For, little has kept Jews away from *Eretz Yisroel* more than material-istic concerns, especially in this day and age of Jewish affluence among the nations of the world.

This suits the *Sitra Achra* just fine, to whom *Kibbutz Golios* means his complete and utter demise, something that Balak, Bilaam, and Amalek understood well.[9] Thus, any hint of *Kibbutz Golios* forces him into a mode of attack that results in our viewing *Eretz Yis-roel* as a place that is materialistically "unsafe."

---

[7] *Bamidbar* 25:1.

[8] *Pri Tzaddik, Mattos* 2.

[9] Seemingly better than we Jews understand. Often our ene-mies have observed and understood the Jewish people better than the Jewish people themselves.

Indeed, the Vilna Gaon wrote how when he prompted *aliyah* to further the goal of *Kibbutz Golios* in his day, he met with serious opposition from many sides. He chalked up all the opposition to the age-old *Sitra Achra* fighting for its life, and pointed out that the *gematria* of "Amalek" (when each letter is spelled as it sounds) equals the *gematria* of "*Sitra Achra*,"[10] and taught that:

> The main point of our work in bringing about the ingathering of the exiles is the war against Amalek. (*Kol HaTor*, Chapter 1)

Therefore, one has to know from the outset that when it comes to regaining and settling *Eretz Yisroel*, it is going to be a battle—a *spiritual* battle, a *physical* battle, and maybe an *actual* battle. *Eretz Yisroel* represents the key to the Final Redemption, and as such it spells the end of the *Sitra Achra's* existence, and therefore, he will invoke whatever abilities he has to prevent the return of the *entire* Jewish nation to the borders of the land of our fathers.

However, return to her borders we must, and, by a certain *fixed* date.[11] It was built into the master plan for Creation long before there was even a Jewish peo-

---

[10] *Kol HaTor*, Chapter 1.
[11] As mentioned already, there is a final, immutable date.

ple. But, what of the *Sitra Achra* and his fight for survival? The answer comes, once again, from the realm
of *Sod*, and may even help to explain the apparent
backwardness of all that has transpired over the last
100 years.

The *Arizal* revealed:

> For a great soul to leave the [realm of spiritual
> impurity[12]], you should know, it must be done
> with *trickery* and *scheming*…Thus, you will
> find that many great souls have come in the bod-
> ies of simpletons, and sometimes even in the
> children of evil people, just as Avraham was born
> from Terach…It was similar with respect to
> Dovid *HaMelech*, who only left the [the realm of
> spiritual impurity] at the time of the incident
> mentioned by *Chazal* on the *verse, "Behold, in
> iniquity was I fashioned"* (*Tehillim* 51:7; *Yalkut*

---

[12] Kabbalah explains that after the sin of Adam *HaRishon*, most
of the souls that were incorporated within his own soul, and
which were to be those of future mankind, left him as a result.
They "fell" into a spiritual domain referred to as the "*Klipos*,"
which is often translated as "encrustations." The main point is
that it is there that the souls remain—on various different levels—until the time comes for particular souls to enter the
world, usually after a long process that is described in detail in
Sha'ar HaGilgulim. In short, the *Klipos* are a counter-spiritual
force that God created to support the concept of free-will and
to be a part of the rectification process of the souls.

HaMakiri, Tehillim 69). For, he had thought, his father Yishai had fathered him through a concubine, whereas in truth it had been through [Yishai's] actual wife . . . However, had it not been for all of this the [spiritual impurities] would never have let him leave. This is also the reason for the episodes of Tamar, Rus, Rachav the prostitute, all the souls of converts, all the kings from Dovid, and *Moshiach* who will have come from Rus the Moabite and the union of Yehudah and Tamar. Rebi Akiva himself was the son of converts who descended from Sisera. This is the trickery and scheming that The Holy One, Blessed is He, uses against the [spiritual impurities] in order to free a soul exploited amongst them. (*Sha'ar HaGilgulim*, Introduction 38)

In order to put these remarkable words into perspective, we have to reiterate certain fundamentals. First of all, God created the world, sustains it, and maintains it. He is the only power within Creation, as we proclaim when we say the six words of the "*Shema*" each day. No matter what occurs in history, for good or for bad, it will always be a function of His will, either in an *obvious* or in a *hidden* way.

On the other hand, God made man, and endowed him with free-will. He made Creation for man and in such a way as to support the concept of free-will, establishing it based upon certain rules such as cause-and-effect. All that exists within Creation, whether we appreciate it or not, is in order to give man the opportunity to make free-will decisions. For this reason, God Himself interacts with His Creation *within* the guidelines His infinite wisdom deemed necessary to satisfy this purpose of existence.

Thus, even though God can bring about results any way He wishes, for the sake of man and free-will, He will often bring them about in what appears to man in a "backwards" manner. The quote above from *Sha'ar HaGilgulim* is an example of this.

Now, based upon what we have just learned from the *Arizal*, and recalling the crucial insight provided by the *Shem M'Shmuel*, we can ask the following question: *What would have happened had Eretz Yisroel been returned to the hands of the Torah world, and been developed as a Torah nation from the outset?*

Certainly that would have been the ideal, and it is what the Vilna Gaon and the Chassidic masters had hoped and tried with great self-sacrifice to actually bring about. And, when *Moshiach* finally arrives, may it be in our time, that is precisely what will occur.

Nevertheless, it would have been a direct and overt invitation to the *Sitra Achra*, whose very existence depends upon holding off the Final Redemption, to do battle as well. Assuming that masses of Jews would have heeded the call to return to the Land and build a Torah state, what would the *Sitra Achra* have done?

Everything he *could* do to foil the plan, as he had already done to the religious *yishuvim* that begun in the early days of the students of the Vilna Gaon. Their survival and accomplishments had been nothing short of miraculous, given the adversity they had to contend with. The head-on approach, when it comes to promoting redemption and return to *Eretz Yisroel*, only serves to instigate the *Sitra Achra* against those carrying it out, and his methods of obstruction are many, varied, and quite destructive.

For a while the *Sitra Achra* had been successful. For millennia, *Eretz Yisroel* had remained vacant of thriving Jewish communities, and the land lay in ru-ins—physically and spiritually. For thousands of years, the *Sitra Achra* had been able to count *Eretz Yisroel* as one of his possessions:

> The war against Amalek is from generation to generation…and is against three types of foes: a) Amalek of the heart, that is, the evil inclination and vices; b) the spirit of Amalek, the general one, the *Satan* who destroys and the adversary of Israel. This is *Samae"l* and his hosts. His main power is in the gates of Jerusalem, when its

lands are desolate. (*Kol HaTor*, Chapter 6)

However, history is only meant to last 6000 years, and according to the Holy *Zohar*, the world as we know it is already destined to undergo serious physical and spiritual transformation at least 210 years in advance of Year 6000.[13] And *that* period can only begin after 40 years of *Kibbutz Golios*, the ingathering of the exiles from the four corners of the world, which, according to this calculation, would have begun in the year 1990.

As we know from many sources, the Final Redemption is a long, ongoing process that, according to the Vilna Gaon, began in his time:

> The Gaon merited being the light of *Moshiach Ben Yosef*, in order to promote the ingathering of the exiles and to reveal the hints in the Torah regarding the footsteps of the *Moshiach Ben Yosef*. He was therefore sent down from Heaven...After many of his students had promised him to go to *Tzion* and begin working there on gathering in the exiles when the awakening starts from below, with the help of God, the Gaon revealed to them all the steps of the beginning of the Redemption. (*Kol HaTor*, Ch. 1)

---

[13] See Chapter Four.

But when it comes to matters of redemption, at least in the early stages, it never pays to confront the *Sitra Achra* head on. Rather, he must be dealt with cleverly and in a scheming manner; he must be given the impression that what he fears most is *not* actually happening, when in fact it *is* happening. And then we have to pray and hope that he doesn't catch on until it is too late to do anything about it.

That said, what better way to do *this* than through those who are not only *irreligious*, but even *anti-Torah?* What better disguise for *Kibbutz Golios* can there be than the development of a "Jewish" country so intent upon shedding its traditional identity that it leaves God out of its proclamation of statehood?[14] What could the *Sitra Achra* have found dangerous to his survival in letting secular Zionist leaders[15] begin a state that could have easily been in Uganda, for all they cared?

---

[14] Rabbi Berel Wein writes, "Zionism redefined the Jewish people. It was no longer a people based upon Sinai and revelation, upon Torah and tradition. It was rather to be a people with a shared "culture," this said "culture" being non-Jewish in origin and outlook, and dedicated to a goal of nationhood for the sake of nationhood itself" (*Triumph Of Survival: Political Zionism*, page 240).

[15] Including its principle leader, a man whose connection to Judaism was so weak that his first answer to anti-Semitism was complete conversion of the entire Jewish nation to Christianity (*Compete Diaries of Theodor Herzl*, page 7).

"Nope, no sign of redemption here," the *Sitra Achra* must have gloated to himself, as he followed the development of the tiny, secular state of Israel.

After all, the *Sitra Achra*, as an angel of God, knows the expectations of his Master: a Torah-state, and daily sanctification of the holy Name of God. As of 1948, He was getting just the opposite,[16] and therefore, the *Sitra Achra* found no reason to interfere in the process and left modern Israeli history to run its secular course.

Until, *that is,* around 1990. Around 1990, as secular Zionism began to wane, the *Sitra Achra* woke up

---

[16] This itself may be a trigger for the Final Redemption, albeit somewhat vicariously. For, as the prophet said: " *I scattered them among the nations and they were dispersed among the lands; according to their acts did I judge them. They came among the nations where they came, and they desecrated My holy Name when it was said of them, 'These are the people of God, but they departed His land.' I took pity on My holy Name, which the House of Israel had desecrated among the nations where they came. Therefore, say to the House of Israel: Thus said the Lord, God: It is not for your sake that I act, O House of Israel, but for My Holy Name that you have desecrated among the nations where you came. I will sanctify My great Name that is desecrated among the nations, that you have desecrated among them; then the nations will know that I am God— the word of the Lord, God—when I become sanctified through you before their eyes, I will take you from the nations and gather you from all the lands, and I will bring you to your own soil." (Yechezkel 36:19-24)*

and saw the last 50 years from an entirely different perspective. As he looked around, *yes*, he saw a predominantly secular state becoming even more so with each passing day. However, he also saw how many thriving Torah communities had taken root in the Holy Land, as well.

Realizing, perhaps for the first time, that God had pulled the wool over his eyes for the last 100 years, bringing about *Kibbutz Golios* and the Final Redemption under the guise of just the opposite, he put the brakes on. All of a sudden, he focussed all of his power on making *Eretz Yisroel* an undesirable place to live, and has worked tirelessly to make Torah survival in the Holy Land as difficult as possible.

And, as we learn from the story of Iyov, he has no problem turning the world upside down to accomplish this end, either. After all, he is fighting for survival, and nothing is more dangerous than a man, or rather an angel, in desperation.

However, for the *Sitra Achra*, if we are truly as far along the path to the Final Redemption as it seems we may be, it may be too little too late. Nevertheless, for those of us living at this time, it may prove to be the biggest test of our lives, as we are forced to evaluate and re-evaluate our connection to the Land and Jewish destiny. Indeed, in a masterful attempt to fool the *Sitra Achra*, so many of the Jewish people may have become fooled along the way as well.

As the *Arizal* reveals, it is a perception problem going back all the way to the days of Yosef and his brothers:

When the ten spies went out to spy the land, the souls of the ten corresponding tribes came into them, the actual sons of Ya'akov. This is the *sod* of what Yosef told [his brothers], *"You are spies"* (*Bereishis* 42:9), alluding that in the future their souls would go into the spies. This is also the *sod* of, *"All of them were heads of the Children of Israel"* (*Bamidbar* 13:3), because they were actually the original ancestors of the Children of Israel. Therefore, it does not call them "heads of thousands of Israel," but rather, "heads of the Children of Israel." After they decided to speak evil about the land and wanted to tell Moshe it was a mistake to go there, the souls of the tribes left them...This is the reason why it says, *"They returned from spying the land at the end of forty days"* (*Bamidbar* 13:25), and then it mentions that they went: *"They went and they came to Moshe and Aharon"* (Ibid. 26); it should only have mentioned that they came. Though *Chazal* explain this according to the simple understanding, that "their going" was similar to their "coming" (*Sotah* 35a), according to *Sod* the "going" refers to the souls of the tribes that left them when they returned from spying the land with an evil report. Thus, the word "coming" refers only to the spies themselves, who came without the souls of the tribes. However, Caleiv and Yehoshua retained theirs: Ephraim ben Yosef was in Yehoshua, and Yehudah was in Caleiv, since they did not sin. This is what it says, *"Yehoshua bin Nun and Caleiv ben Yefuneh survived from these men who went"* (*Bamidbar* 14:38), that is: these remained alive from the level of the souls of the tribes of their fathers who were in them; they did not leave them after they returned. Hence, just as they were with them when they had gone, so too were they with them upon returning. This is what *"survived from the men who went"* means. Therefore, "these men" refers to Ephraim and Yehudah who were with them in their going, as it says, *"who went,"* to indicate that these survived from those who went, unlike those whose coming was not like their going. (*Sha'ar HaGilgulim*, Chapter 36)

In other words, what went wrong with the spies can be traced back to the brothers' misjudgment and mistreatment of Yosef. And, what's even more amazing is that the brothers had rejected Yosef because they had thought that God had also rejected him, even though just the opposite had been true.[17]

Therefore, they went about their business of disposing of Yosef right under the nose of God. Probably because of the success they had in doing so, they believed that God had approved of their actions. Nev-

---

[17] The *Ramban* asks: Why does the Torah use the same word with respect to the spies at the beginning of the *parsha*, "*See the land* (וּרְאִיתֶם)—*what is it?*" (*Bamidbar* 13:18), and the *mitzvah* of *tzitzis* at the end of the *parsha*: "*It shall constitute tzitzis for you, and you shall see* (וּרְאִיתֶם) *it (the techeles thread) and remember them (mitzvos) and do them*" (*Bamidbar* 15:39)? The *Ramban* answers: To make the point that the failure of the spies was what the *mitzvah* of *tzitzis* helps to rectify. The Talmud teaches: Rebi Meir used to say, "What is unique about blue (*techeles*) from all other colors? Blue is like the sea, and the sea is like the sky, and the sky is like the Throne of Glory, as it says, "*And under His feet was the likeness of sapphire, brickwork, and it was like the essence of heaven in purity*" (*Shemos* 24:10), and it says, "*The appearance of sapphire stone in the likeness of a throne*" (*Yechezkel* 1:26). (*Menachos* 43b). In other words, explains the *Ramban*, a Jew is supposed to be able to look at a single strand of blue thread which he *can* see, and from that build a connection to the Throne of Glory which he *cannot*, and as a result, remember all of the *mitzvos*. As we remind ourselves each Chanukah, we are a people who believe and survive because we know that nothing in this world is really what it seems to be on the surface, and therefore, requires investigation. Thus, from this we learn than the spies were supposed to have looked at *Eretz Yisroel*, but not just on the surface, but past the physical aspects of the land into its awesomely holy nature. This approach to viewing *Eretz Yisroel* would have immediately resulted in a love of the land.

er once did it cross their minds that they were setting up their own demise, not Yosef's. Not once did they consider that by degrading Yosef they were in fact sending him on his way to greatness, at their own expense too.

Hashgochah Pratis can be very tricky indeed.

If only the brothers had known THEN that by selling Yosef they were really selling themselves out. However, that revelation was at first slow to come, until Yosef finally revealed that it was him behind the clothing of the second-in-command of Egypt, and to whom they had reverently bowed.

The story begs the question: Why *did* the brothers not recognize Yosef, in spite of all the signs he gave them? For, as Yehudah had told a distressed Ya'akov, who questioned their judgment:

> *"Why did you treat me badly, telling the man that you have another brother?"*
>
> *They answered, "The man persistently asked about us and about our relatives . . ." (Bereishis* 43:6-7)

ABOUT US . . . RELATIVES: Even the [type of] wood of our cribs he revealed to us. (*Rashi*)

—information only a brother could know.

However, as the *Ohr HaChaim HaKodesh* explains, the possibility that Yosef could have been a slave and then rise to the heights of Egyptian power was beyond their ability to conceive, in spite of his dreams of greatness.[18] So greatly had they misjudged Yosef that they had become blind to his true potential and greatness, and to how important he could be to God.

Sound familiar? In fact, Yosef particularly is connected to the whole concept of redemption, as the Midrash teaches:

All that happened to Yosef happened to *Tzion*. (*Tanchuma, Vayigash* 10)

In fact, the *gematria* of "Yosef" and "Tzion" are exactly the same: 156. And, through Yosef's own ancestors *at the time of the spies*, we learn how intricately connected Yosef's being was to *Eretz Yisroel:*

The daughters of Tzelofchad—the son of Cheifer, the son of Gilad, the son of Machir, the son of Menashe, from the family of Menashe, the son of Yosef—approached. These are the names of his daughters: Machlah, No'ah, Chaglah, Milkah, and Tirtzah. (Bamidbar 27:1)

---

[18] *Bereishis* 42:8.

FROM THE FAMILY OF MENASHE, THE SON OF YOSEF: Why did it have to mention this, since it already said "the son of Menashe"? To tell you that Yosef loved the Land, as it says, *"Bring my bones up"* (*Bereishis* 50:25), and that his "daughters" also loved the land, as it says, *"Give us our possession"* (*Bamidbar* 27:4). (*Rashi*)

Small wonder then that it is his descendant, *Moshiach* BEN YOSEF, who will be responsible for bringing the exiles back to *Eretz Yisroel*:

All the steps, all the rules and details concerning the period from the beginning of the Redemption until its conclusion, which include the ingathering of the exiles and the settlement of the Holy Land—all these are the task of the first *Moshiach*, *Moshiach Ben Yosef*. (*Kol HaTor*, Chapter 1)

Do Jews today look at *Eretz Yisroel* as the brothers once viewed Yosef? Will *Eretz Yisroel*, at the End-of-Days, reveal its true self and proclaim, *"I AM ERETZ YISROEL,"* at which point millions of Jews will reel backwards in shock, speechless, wondering how they could have ever misjudged the land of their Forefathers, and the opportunity of the time? Recall the words of the *Arizal*:

In the future, Moshe himself will reincarnate and return in the last generation, as it says, *"you will lie with your fathers and rise up"* (*Devarim* 31:16). However, in the final generation, the *"Dor HaMidbar"* (Generation of the Desert) will also reincarnate with the *Erev Rav* (Mixed Multitude), and this is what the *verse* also says, *"this people will rise up."* Hence, there is not a single generation in which Moshe *Rabbeinu* does not return *b'sod*, *"The sun rises and the sun sets"* (*Koheles* 1:5) and, *"One generation goes and another comes"* (*Koheles* 1:4), in order to rectify that generation. Thus, the Generation of the Desert along with the *Erev Rav* reincarnate in the final generation, *"like in the days of leaving Egypt"* (*Michah* 7:15). (*Sha'ar HaGilgulim*, Chapter 20)

That would make the end of Jewish history just like its beginning. Like "bookends" at two extremes of history, the 210 years of resurrection mirror the 210 years of Egyptian exile,[19] and the 40 years of ingathering mirror the 40 years of wandering:[20]

---

[19] Which, the *Arizal* says was supposed to have had the same effect as *Techiyas HaMeisim*, returning mankind back to its state before Adam *HaRishon's* sin.

[20] America has been called a spiritual *midbar* (desert) by Torah Jews.

1523-1313: 210 years in Egypt
1313-1273: 40 years of "ingathering"

1990-2030: 40 years of ingathering
2030-2240: 210 years of resurrection

The rest of history in-between, from 1273 BCE until 1990 CE—3,263 years—has just been a passage of time from "Point A" to "Point B."

A hint to all of this is in the very name we give to the end of history: *Keitz HaYomim*—End Of Days. However, grammatically-speaking, it should be, *"Keitz Yomim"*; the former translates more literally as, "end of THE days." But to which days *specifically* does this refer?

The answer to this question is implied by the following *verse*:

> *[God] said to Avram, "Know that your descendants will be strangers in a land that is not theirs, and [the host nation] will enslave them, and afflict them for 400 years." (Bereishis 15:13)*

According to this prophecy, the Jewish people were supposed to have been in Egypt for 400 years, as foretold to Avraham, not 210 years. However, since the *verse* did not actually name Egypt as the place of exile, it was left open to count the 400 years from the birth of Yitzchak, instead of from when Ya'akov and his family went down to Egypt.[21]

However, the simplest reading of the verse implies that the same nation that would enslave Avraham's descendants would be the same nation to host them for the entire period of 400 years. And, therefore, even though there is a way to make history consistent with the *verse* by counting from the birth of Yitzchak *Avinu* until the time of redemption, technically, we left Egypt 190 years *early*.

Why early? Because, as the commentators point out, the Jewish people had descended to the 49th level of spiritual impurity, at which point we had been teetering on the verge of spiritual oblivion. By the time God sent the first plague against the Egyptian people, the Jewish people had just been short of becoming irredeemable; only because God stepped in did we turn the tide back in the direction of redemption.

The question is, what happened to the remaining 190 years? Did God simply forgive the debt?

The answer is, *No*. Instead, the remaining 190 years were spread out over the rest of Jewish history. If so, then *Keitz HaYomim* would not only mean the *end of days*, but the end of *THOSE days*—the days of Egyptian servitude that we left unfinished. In other words, even though we left Egypt physically in the

---

[21] In *Parashas Vayigash*.

year 2448/1313 BCE, spiritually, we have been leaving it ever since. No wonder the *Haggadah Shel Pesach* tells us:

> Every year, we read in the *Haggadah Shel Pesach* that each Jew must look at himself as if he too left Egypt.

In every generation, we *ARE* leaving Egypt, little-by-little, until *Moshiach* finally arrives, signaling that the Egyptian exile has finally come to an end.

And as if to make the point perfectly clear, the *gematria* of "*keitz*" (.e) is 190—precisely the amount of years that remained in the Egypt exile. Thus, the entire phrase means: the end of the days of the 190 years. This would help to explain why the Egyptian exile is considered to be very different from the other four—Babylonia, Median, Greek, and Roman—exile.

It is fascinating how we have come to believe that ancient Jewish history was just that, *ancient*, only to find that it is *alive*, *well*, and the *true* undercurrent for all that is happening today.

> The exodus from Egypt liberated only one out of five Jews—and some say one out of every fifty—because all those who were bound to Egypt and did not want to depart died in the three days of darkness and were not privileged to leave. That

is, only those who desired redemption with all their hearts were redeemed. The Final Redemption, likewise, depends upon our yearning. (*Ohr Yechezkel.*[22] *(Emunas HaGeulah,* p. 288)

---

[22] See *Sanhedrin* 111a, where it says: Rava said, "It will be likewise in *Yemos HaMoshiach,* as it says, *'She will dwell there as in the days of her youth, and as on the day of her ascent from Egypt'.*" Rashi explains, from all the 60 myriads [that will be alive in advance of *Moshiach's* arrival], only two will survive.

Alillus

eleven

THE WORD ALILLUS is a *Hebrew* word. The question is, what does it mean, what does it have to do with the current issue, and why is it such an important Kabbalistic concept to know in everyday life?

It translates as "likelihood," but it can also mean: plot, deed, act, scene, false charge, libel,[1] or pretext. All of these terms fit the bill, as the following *midrash* relates:

> *"Go and see the works of God, awesome in deed toward mankind." (Tehillim* 66:5): Go and see how when The Holy One, Blessed is He, created

---

[1] A blood libel is *"alillus dumm."*

the world, He created the Angel of Death on the *first* day...Man, however, was created on the *sixth* day, and yet death was blamed on him. To what is this similar? To a man who wants to divorce his wife and writes her a *Get*, after which he returns home holding the *Get*, looking for a pretext[2] to give it to her. He tells her, *"Prepare me a drink."*

She does, and taking it from her he says, *"Here is your Get."*

She says, *"What is this?"*

He then tells her, *"Leave my house since you made me a warm drink,"* to which she replies,

"How did you know in advance that I would prepare you a warm drink that you were able to write a Get and come home with it?"

So too Adam said to The Holy One, Blessed is He,

"Master of the Universe! The Torah was with You for 2000 years before You even created the world...And yet it instructs, *'This is the law when a man will die in a tent'* (*Bamidbar* 19:14). If You had not *already* decided that death should be in Creation, would You have written this? Rather, You were just looking for a pretext to blame death on me!"

---

[2] The Hebrew word is "alillah."

This is what is meant by *"awesome in deed."*
(*Tanchuma, Vayaishev* 4)

Awesome, that is, as in *beyond comprehension* and *appreciation*.

At first glance, this is a profoundly perplexing *midrash*. Its clear implication is that man can be held accountable for results he cannot control. However, a short but crucial declaration by the Talmud, seemingly, sets matters straight:

> The Holy One, Blessed is He, does not come *b'trunia* (*Rashi: b'alillah*) with His creations. (*Avodah Zarah* 3a)

In other words, God does not play games with His creations; He is not some cruel dictator looking for ways to unduly cause trouble for His constituents. Rather, He is a benevolent Creator Who may chastise His children, but always for their *own* good, not *His*.

However, that was not what the *Midrash* taught, and the truth is, it is not what the Talmud itself teaches elsewhere:

> What did The Holy One, Blessed is He, do? He brought suffering to Chizkiah and told Yeshayahu, "Go and visit the sick," as it says, *"In those days Chizkiah became ill to the point of*

death; and Yeshayahu the son of Amotz, the prophet, came and said to him, 'So says God, Lord of Hosts: Command your house for you shall die and not live.' " (*Yeshayahu* 38:1).

"Why do I deserve such a severe punishment?" asked Chizkiah.

"Because," answered Yeshayahu, *"you have not had children."*

"But I saw through prophecy that I will have evil children."

"What business have you with kavshei Rachmanah?" Yeshayahu answered. (*Brochos* 10a)

Kavshei Rachmanah refers to the hidden matters of God, the aspects of His Divine Providence that we cannot fathom.

Chizkiah *HaMelech*, like every male, had a *mitzvah* to procreate. However, God had already revealed to him that when he would have children, one would become king and lead the country astray.[3] After bringing the Jewish people to incredible heights of spiritual perfection, what was such a righteous king like Chizkiah to do to avoid such a terrible catastrophe? The only thing he could do was to abstain from having children.

However, in spite of his holy intentions, for his

---

[3] Which Menashe ben Chizkiah actually did for 33 years (II *Melachim* 21:1).

decision he became deserving of death. And though Chizkiah defended his actions, Yeshayahu countered by saying that, just because we don't like what God has planned does not mean we can change it by avoiding our obligations. We simply have to accept that God *always* knows best, and runs His world in a way that we cannot always fathom, according to something called *alillus*.

This is the same message that God gave to Moshe on top of Mt. Sinai when he ascended to receive the Torah. The Talmud says:

> When Moshe ascended on High, he found The Holy One, Blessed is He, sitting and tying crowns onto the letters.[4] He said before Him, *"Master of the Universe! What are you doing."*
>
> He answered him, *"There is a man who will come after many generations and Akiva ben Yosef will be his name. In the future, he will elucidate every point and mounds of law."*[5]
>
> He said to Him, *"Master of the Universe! Show him to me."*
>
> He told him, *"Turn around."*

---

[4] The lines that extent out from many of the letters in a *Sefer Torah*.

[5] In other words, he will be gifted with a special ability to see in these special demarcations in the Written Torah hints to laws known from the Oral Law.

Moshe turned around and sat at the back in the eighth row.[6] However, when Moshe did not recognize what they were discussing, he became distressed until a student asked, *"Rebi, from where do we learn that?"*[7]

Rebi Akiva answered, *"It is a halachah that goes back to Moshe at Mt. Sinai."*

With this answer, Moshe was calmed and returned to The Holy One, Blessed is He, and said, *"Master of the Universe! You have one such as he and You wish to give the Torah through me!"*

God answered, *"Silence! This is what I planned to do!"*

He said to Him, *"Master of the Universe! You showed me his Torah, now show me his reward!"*

He told him, *"Turn around."*

He turned around and saw them weighing his flesh in the market place,[8] and said, *"Master of*

---

[6] It was a prophecy of a class given by the future Rebi Akiva.

[7] Not recognizing the law, Moshe was concerned that the Torah tradition he was about to learn and teach would eventually be broken. However, once he heard Rebi Akiva answer that the law could be traced back to Moshe at Mt. Sinai, he understood that God would eventually teach it to him and that in the prophecy, Rebi Akiva had already learned it.

[8] After having been tortured to death by the Romans for teaching Torah in public (*Brochos* 61b).

*the Universe! This is Torah and this is its re-
ward?!"*

He answered him, *"Silence! This is what I
planned to do!"* (Menachos 29b)

Another difficult *midrash*, but this time from the
Talmud. The question is, what's the *pshat* here? The
Pshat is, it seems from the Talmud, that God does
many things in history that we simply can't understand. *Alillus*. In fact, sometimes He allows events to
occur that appear so incredibly evil that we have to be
taught to say, *"All that God does is for the good"* (Brochos 60b), and we have to be told:

*Many are the thoughts of man, but the will of
God is what prevails. (Mishlei 19:21)*

Countless times throughout our long and ardu-
ous history, those who have been unable to believe
these statements have abandoned the idea of Divine
Providence. And, in many tragic cases, feeling abandoned by God they have abandoned the notion of
God altogether.

But that's only *Pshat*—and perhaps *Remez* and
Drush as well. On the level of *Sod*, the question is often greatly whittled down, as we saw earlier with story
of Iyov. Nevertheless, even the level of *Sod* can fall
short when it comes to undoing *alillus*, as God Him-

self told Moshe *Rabbeinu:*

> *No one can see My face because no man can
> see Me and live! (Shemos* 33:20)

Face? God has a *face?* Well, not in everyday
terms, but *conceptually*-speaking. For, what is a face
but a way to reveal the inner essence of a person,
which is why the Hebrew word for face is *"panim,"*
derived from the word that means "inside." If so, then
what was God actually telling Moshe?

The dialogue had occurred after the sin of the
golden calf, after Moshe had rid the camp of the per-
petrators and returned to the top of Mt. Sinai to mitigate the punishment for those who remained. Successful at invoking God's mercy, Moshe then took advantage of the situation and asked God:

> *"Please show me Your ways." (Shemos* 33:13)

According to the Talmud, this is what was really
behind Moshe *Rabbeinu's* request:

> Moshe wanted to know the ways of The Holy
> One, Blessed is He…He asked Him, "Master of
> the Universe! Why are there righteous people
> who prosper and righteous people who suffer;
> evil people who prosper and evil people who

suffer?" (*Brochos* 7a)

It was basically the same question that Moshe had asked regarding the terrible death of Rebi Akiva:

"Master of the Universe! This is Torah and this is its reward?!"

It is also the underlying premise of Yeshayahu's answer to Chizkiah *HaMelech's* decision to avoid having offspring, and, it is the principle upon which the *midrash* quoted at the beginning of this chapter is based. God's answer to Moshe:

"I will be gracious to whom I will be gracious, and show My mercy to whom I will show My mercy." (Shemos 33:19)

That is, even if we can't understand why.[9] For, sometimes things happen in everyday life that don't have to do with everyday life. Sometimes, the original purpose for Creation, rooted high up in the *Sefiros* where no human mind can go, demands certain rectifications to occur down here in order to keep Creation

---

[9] *Brochos* 7a.

on track and on time.[10]

And this, essentially, is what God told Moshe when He said:

"No one can see My face because no man can see Me and live"! (Shemos 33:20)

That is, the answer to your questions are at levels of Divine will too sublime and intense for the human mind to handle.

Indeed, in Kabbalah, "face" and *"machsha-vah"* are Kabbalistic terms for very high levels in the *Sefiros.*[11] This idea is the basis of all Kabbalah, and the details are both awesome in number and complexity. However, the main point here is that everything that happens in history is a function of God's will, which becomes filtered—*and therefore more hidden from man*—on its way down into our everyday world.

Moshe, in Heaven already, requested a perception of God's will on a much higher, far more sublime plane. He wanted to perceive it on the level where all

---

[10] The spiritual system that God created to "filter" His light down to Creation. They are a series of spiritual "transformers"—ten in general (*Keser, Chochmah, Binah, Chesed, Gevuros, Tifferes, Netzach, Hod, Yesod*, and *Malchus*)—between God and man, each one receiving light from the level above it, reducing it somewhat, and then passing it on to the level below it.

[11] For example, *"Machshavah"* is the level of the *Binah* of *Arich Anpin,* which corresponds to the level of *Keser.*

the myriads of historical details merge into a single Divine expression of will for all of existence. On that level, everything makes *perfect* sense in the most *perfect* way.

However, as God told Moshe, it is also a level of Divine light that is far too intense for any human mind, even one as great as Moshe *Rabbeinu's*. Human exposure to such light could only result in instant death and therefore, it was denied to Moshe. Thus, he was left with the question with which he began.

For the time being, that is.

For, though some of the *alillus* will not be answered until the World-to-Come, sometimes answers come within a millennium, a century, or even a single decade. Many will come instantly the moment *Moshiach* arrives and rights our upside-down world. Some are available already, for those who venture into the realm of *Sod* in the right way for the proper reasons.

In the meantime, the question of *alillus* itself is a partial answer, especially when it comes to the issue of *Eretz Yisroel* at this late stage of history. Between the negative events that occur here daily, and prevailing attitudes towards *Eretz Yisroel* of Jews abroad, so much just doesn't make sense, *at least to us.* And, as the world becomes increasingly unstable and the Jewish position even more defenseless, it is hard not to feel vulnerable.

Thus it says in *Sefer Iyov,* the very book of *alil-*

lus:

> *"Did you ever in your life command the morning, or teach the dawn its place, to grasp the edges of the earth and shake the wicked from it?" (Iyov 38:12-13)*

which *Rashi* explains to mean:

> In your life, did you ever command the corners of the earth to be taken like a man grabs the corners of a garment, to shake it? In the future, I will grasp [the earth's] corners and shake out the evil people... *(Rashi)*

And, how will God do *that* if not through *alillus?* *Alillus* tests and stretches every human being's level of faith in God's Divine Providence. It is the apparent randomness and success of evil that pushes our minds and hearts to their limits, like gravity tugging at a person who desperately hangs from a rope. Philosophically, letting go means the abandonment of God and Torah, God forbid.

If that is the case, then shouldn't we stop evaluating the happenings of today on a superficial level, according to *Pshat* only? Should we not reconsider our position with respect to ideas and realities that the Torah has always held important and dear, as uncomfortable as it may be to do so? After all, it is the *Sitra Achra* that we want to fool, not *ourselves*.

Even the issue of the *Gedolei HaTorah*—the main Torah leaders—not promoting *aliyah* in any direct way brings to mind certain sources that put this issue into perspective. For example, there is the *midrash* quoted earlier in Chapter Eight regarding Pinchas' act of zealousness. There is also an account from the Talmud from the time of the Roman siege of Jerusalem:

> When [Rebi Yochanan ben Zakkai] arrived [at the Roman camp],[12] he said, *"Peace unto you, king! Peace unto you, king!"*
>
> [Vespasian] answered him, *"You are now de-*

---

[12] As the Roman's laid siege to the walled city of Jerusalem to force the surrender of the resident Jewish community, there was an internal disagreement as to how to respond to the plight. The division was between the Torah scholars of that time, led by the great Rabbi Yochanan ben Zakkai, and the non-religious Jews, led by his nephew. Rabbi Yochanan ben Zakkai saw the futility of the situation and decided that survival of the Jewish people was better served by surrendering to the powerful Roman army just beyond the walls. The *Bironim*, as the other group was called, wanted only to stand their ground and fight to the finish. They were even prepared to murder any Jew willing to leave the besieged city and bargain with the Romans. Nevertheless, Rabbi Yochanan defied the ban and risked his life to leave the city and meet with the conquering Roman general to negotiate the surrender.

serving of death twice. Firstly, I am not the king and yet you have called me king. Secondly, if I am the king, why did you not come to me earlier?"

He answered, *"I called you king because one day you will be, for, if you weren't a king then Jerusalem would not have been given over to you, as it says, 'And the Levanon will fall by a mighty (adir)' (Yeshayahu 10:34). Now, 'mighty' (adir) refers to a king, as it says, 'And the leader (adir) shall be of themselves' (Yirmiyahu 30:21). 'Levanon' refers to the Temple, as it says, 'This goodly mountain and the Levanon' (Devarim 3:25). As to your question, that if you were a king why did I not come to you earlier, it was because the rebels among us prevented me from leaving."*

However, Vespasian responded, *"If there is a barrel full of honey and a serpent is around it, is it not proper to break the barrel because of the serpent?"*[13]

Rabbi Yochanan could not answer. Rav Yosef, and others say Rebi Akiva applied the following verse to him, *"Who makes wise men retreat and makes their knowledge foolish"* (Yeshayahu 44:25). [For, Rebi Yochanan] should have an-

---

[13] Why didn't *you* destroy the city to get rid of the rebels?

swered, "It is better to take tongs and remove the serpent from the barrel and kill it, and leave the barrel intact."[14] (*Gittin* 56b)

A troubling tract of Talmud, one that can easily be abused and throw into question, *God forbid,* the authority of Torah leaders. Is not *Emunas Chachamim*—faith in Torah leaders—based upon our belief that God is with them, assisting our Torah leaders in their decision-making for the best of the Jewish people? How could God have denied Rebi Yochanan such an important answer at such a crucial moment, and how often does this happen in Jewish history?

For some reason, *Rashi* and *Tosfos* do not explain the meaning of the *verse* quoted by Rebi Akiva. However, fortunately, the *Maharsha*[15] does, and as a result brings to light another very important concept. He wrote:

> In other words, the sin of the people of the city was the cause for The Holy One, Blessed is He, to *"make wise men retreat,"* denying them the knowledge to answer. (*Maharsha,* q.v. *Who makes wise men retreat*)

---

[14] That is, why destroy the city when you can extricate the rebels, as I have come to do successfully?

[15] Rabbi Shmuel Edels (1555-1631).

In other words, explains the *Maharsha*, Rabbi Yochanan's silence was not due to any shortcoming of his own. Rather, his inability to answer correctly at that moment was the result of the people he had left behind. Indeed, from elsewhere we see that a Torah leader's Heavenly help is a direct function of the people they lead:

> *"God told Moshe: Go down"* (*Shemos* 32:7); what does *"go down"* mean? Rebi Elazar said, "The Holy One, Blessed is He, told Moshe, 'Descend from your [level of] greatness, for I have given you greatness only for the sake of Israel, and now Israel has sinned.' Immediately, Moshe became weak and he lost the strength to speak." (*Brochos* 32a)

Having said this, we can now ask: If the *Gedolei HaTorah* of today insisted that all the Jews of the Diaspora immediately make *aliyah*, would they be ready and willing to go? Would these Jews extend their faith in the *chachamim* 6000 miles to include living within the borders of *Eretz Yisroel?*

The irony of it all: *alillus* exists to fool the *Sitra Achra* and provide us with the chance to choose redemption and *Eretz Yisroel* of our own volition. However, rather than see through the *alillus*, we are taken aback by it. Thus, we close our minds and hearts to

the centrality of *Eretz Yisroel* and end up denying ourselves the chance to be encouraged by those very
people whose opinions we respect the most. More
alillus.

Then there is the issue of the masses. So few
Jews make *aliyah* compared to those who do not, and
some even return back to *Chutz L'Aretz* from *Eretz
Yisroel*. Indeed, the majority of Jews today probably
have little if any yearning at all to live in *Eretz Yisroel* at
some point in their lifetime.

What does *Sod* have to say about this?

We have already learned that, at the end of days,
the souls of the Jews will be those of the generation of
the spies. We have already been told by the Talmud
that, just like in Egypt, the vast majority of Jews will
miss the point in advance of *Moshiach's* arrival. Now, it
turns out, that one's ability to relate to *Eretz Yisroel*
also depends upon the root of one's soul.

According to the *Arizal*, the "source" from
which human souls are taken is also structured like a
human body, spiritually-speaking.[16] Therefore, just as
there is a head, hair, eyes, a nose, a mouth, and so on,
in a physical body, so too do such levels exist for the
spiritual structure from which souls come.[17]

---

[16] *Sha'ar HaGilgulim* Introduction 3.
[17] In truth, the physical world mirrors the spiritual one, and is
really just a physical *projection* of it.

Thus, there are souls that emanate from the head of this structure, while some come from the eyes of it. Others may have their root in the cheeks, while others come from the ears. In fact, the *Arizal* explains, prior to Adam's sin, *HE* was that structure:

> When Adam *HaRishon* sinned he blemished all the sparks of his *Nefesh*, *Ruach*, and *Neshamah*[18]...The Holy One, Blessed is He, showed him every righteous person who would ever descend from him, from his head, his hair, his neck, his two eyes, and some from his nose...Before the sin, Adam *HaRishon* comprised the souls of all the people of history, which were embodied into the spiritual structure of his very being. When he sinned, he blemished the majority of the sparks of his *Nefesh*, *Ruach*, and *Neshamah*, causing them to become immersed in the depths of spiritual impurity. (*Sha'ar HaGilgulim*, Introduction 3)

This concept, in essence, is the reason for all the differences between people and their life situations. It shows how the root of a person's soul affects his approach and even his leanings in life. It can make him sensitive to certain things that do not concern others,

---

[18] The three lower sections of the five levels of soul.

and vice versa. It can even determine whether some-one will be creative with his hands or with speech.[19]

The upshot of all of this is that, when we look at the Jewish people today, living in various parts of the world and doing different things from each other, we may ask ourselves, *"Why can't he see what I see? Why doesn't he feel what I feel? Why does he reject elements of spirituality that I personally cannot live without?"*

However, we have to realize that the answer is not as simple as we assume it to be. It is not only a function of a *hidden* historical process, but a function of a *hidden* soul as well. And, that goes for the way one relates to God, Torah, the concept of redemption, and *yes*, even to *Eretz Yisroel.*[20] Indeed, sometimes our rejection of certain spiritual realities is *only* on the soul-level, something we have *no* control over, and which can greatly influence how we feel about things without our even understanding why.

Nevertheless, as the *Mussar* giants and Kabbalists have pointed out so poignantly, this is usually the

---

[19] *Sha'ar HaGilgulim,* Introduction 36.

[20] Indeed, the *Leshem* writes that the spies had such difficulty making *aliyah* in their time because of the the root of their souls. More *alillus.* However, adds the *Leshem,* had they overcome their spiritual challenge and accepted *Eretz Yisroel* in spite of their inherent difficulties, the *tikun* would have been enough to bring history to an end and begin the period of *Moshiach.*

very *basis* of our test in life. And, it is precisely our gift of free-will that allows us to make decisions with which, *at first,* we may not be comfortable, but which are really the will of God, and our personal path to *tikun*.

The Race For Time

twelve

BY NO MEANS have we answered all the questions, even after having touched on difficult concepts such as *alillus*. All we have done is present evidence showing the danger of viewing history, especially *current* history, *superficially*. And, we have made a case for how *Sod* is a crucial intellectual key for making sense of this "upside-down" world—for getting our spiritual priorities straight.

The reason we have done even *that* is because we are in a race for time. On one hand, it is a race that began ever since the first man was created;[1] on the

---

[1] The concept of *Moshiach* is in the second *verse* about the spirit of God that *"hovered above the waters"* (*Ba'al HaTurim*).

other hand, it is a race that began much later in time, after the Jewish people were freed from Egypt. It is the race to bring history to an end and usher in the Period of *Moshiach*—before God Himself does it.

There are many verses in *Tanach* that either speak about the time of *Moshiach* or allude to it. And, in some of those verses lie hidden information that could be used even to calculate the precise arrival time of *Moshiach*, as the Talmud says:

> The [Aramaic] translation of the Prophets was composed by Yonason ben Uzziel based upon a tradition from [the prophets] Chaggai, Zechariah, and Malachi. When [he completed it,] *Eretz Yisroel* shook for 400 square miles, and a Heavenly Voice went out saying, "Who is the one who revealed My secrets to man?" Yonason ben Uzziel stood up and said, "I am the one who has revealed Your secrets to man. However, it is known and revealed before You that it was not for my honor or the honor of my father's house, but for Your glory, to prevent controversy in Israel!" He had intended to reveal the translation of the Writings when a Heavenly Voice went out and said, "You have already done enough!" Why? The time of *Moshiach* is in it.[2] (*Megillah* 3a)

---

[2] Specifically in the Book of Daniel.

Nevertheless, there is one *verse* that sums up Jewish history and the race:

Your people will all be righteous; they will inherit the land forever; a shoot of My planting. The smallest will increase a thousandfold, and the youngest into a mighty nation. I, God, will hasten it in its time—b'ittah achishenah. (Yeshayahu 60:21-22)

Asks the Talmud:

Rebi Alexandri said: Rebi Yehoshua ben Levi raised the following contradiction, "It is written, '*I, God, will hasten it in its time*' (*Yeshayahu* 60:22). Now, '*hasten*' and '*in its time*' contradict each other. [Rather, God said,] "If they merit it, I will *hasten* it, but if they do not, then only at the *appointed* time." (*Sanhedrin* 98a)

In other words, there are two possible times for *Moshiach* to arrive: the *last* possible moment, and *early*, which means *any* time in history up until the last possible moment. Thus, the *Rambam* wrote:

I believe with perfect faith in the coming of *Moshiach*, and even though he may tarry, nevertheless, I will wait for him every day, that he will come. (*13 Principles of Faith*)

—because he really *can* come any day, but he must come at some time.

At least once, he almost came early, as the Talmud reveals:

> The Holy One, Blessed is He, was about to make Chizkiah[3] the *Moshiach* and Sancheriv, Gog and Magog. The Attribute of Judgment said before The Holy One, Blessed is He, "Master of the Universe! You did not make Dovid, the king of Israel, *Moshiach*, though he recited many songs and praises. And now You want to make, Chizkiah, for whom You *did* perform great miracles but for which he did not recite song, *Moshiach*?" (*Sanhedrin* 94a)

In fact, some of the calculations for early arrival dates by notable rabbis of the past may not have been wrong, even though *Moshiach* did not arrive in the end. They may have been correct mathematically, that is, according to the *Sefiros*,[4] but being early dates, they

---

[3] Mentioned in the previous chapter.

[4] Since the *Sefiros* act as the script for creation, just as DNA acts as the script for a human body, all that happens in history does so when it does because it is built into a particular *sefirah*, which corresponds to a period of 1000 years.

were also dependent upon the merits of the Jewish people:

> Rebi Yehoshua ben Levi met Eliyahu standing at the entrance of a cave of Rebi Shimon bar Yochai and asked him, "When will *Moshiach* appear?"
>
> He answered, "Go and ask *Moshiach* himself."
>
> "But where can he be found?"
>
> "At the gate of Rome."
>
> "And by what sign [can I recognize him]?"
>
> "He is among the poor people afflicted with wounds. They open *all* their bandages, adjust them, and then redress them all at one time. However, [*Moshiach*] only opens, adjusts, and dresses *one* wound at time, to avoid delay if he is called."
>
> I went to him and said, *"Peace be upon you, my master and teacher,"* and he answered,
>
> *"Peace be with you, Bar Levi."*
>
> I asked him, *"When will the master appear?"*
>
> He answered, *"Today."*
>
> I returned to Eliyahu and asked regarding all that *Moshiach* said, and told him that he said, "Peace be with you, Bar Levi."
>
> Eliyahu said, "I can assure you and your father a share in the World-to-Come."[5]

---

[5] Since he mentioned his name and his father's name as well.

"But he made a fool of me," I told Eliyahu, "because he said that he would come today [but did not]."

Eliyahu answered and said, "The expression *'today'* means the same as it does in the verse, *'Today, if you will listen to His voice.'* " (*Tehillim* 95:7). (*Sanhedrin* 98a)

In other words, Eliyahu the prophet explained to Rebi Yehoshua ben Levi, *Moshiach* had been ready to come *that* particular day, *just as he is every day,* had the Jewish people been ready to receive him. And, not only are there two possible times for *Moshiach's* arrival, but each one affects the way he will arrive:

Rebi Alexandri said: Rebi Yehoshua ben Levi raised the following contradiction, "It says, *'Behold like the clouds of Heaven came one like the son of man'* (*Daniel* 7:13). It is also written, *'Lowly and riding upon a donkey'* (*Zechariah* 9:9). If they merit it, he will come with the clouds of Heaven, but if they do not merit it, he will come upon a donkey." (*Sanhedrin* 98a)

In other words, if the Jewish people merit to bring *Moshiach* early, then it will be according to the best of circumstances. Having returned to Torah and *mitzvos* on our own, *Moshiach* will only have to come and lead the world the final distance to rectification. Peace will already have begun its reign even *before Moshiach* has had a chance to arrive.

However, if the Jewish people do not merit to bring *Moshiach* early, the Talmud warns, it will not be pleasant at the end of history:

> Rav said, "All the dates of redemption have already passed, and now it depends upon repentance and good deeds." Shmuel said, "It is enough that the mourner remains in mourning!"[6] This is like an earlier disagreement: Rebi Eliezer said, "If Israel will repent then they will be redeemed, and if they will not, then they will not be redeemed." Rebi Yehoshua said to him, *"If they do not repent they will not be redeemed?!* Rather, The Holy One, Blessed is He, will cause a king to arise who will make decrees as difficult as Haman's and Israel will [be forced to] repent and return to the right path." (*Sanhedrin* 97b)

This, of course, refers to none other than the war of Gog and Magog, also spoken about by the

---

[6] In other words, all the suffering from thousands of years of exile is enough merit for *Moshiach* to come.

prophets:[7]

> *"It shall come to pass on that day, on the day that Gog shall come against the Land of Israel,"* says the Lord, God, *"My fury shall rise up . . . And in My jealousy, in the fire of My anger, I have spoken—surely on that day there will be a great shaking in Eretz Yisroel. The fish of the sea and the birds of the sky and the beasts of the field, and all the creeping things that creep upon the earth, and all the people who are upon the face of the earth, shall shake at My Presence; the mountains shall be destroyed, the steep places shall fall, and every wall will fall to the ground."* (Yechezkel 38:18-20)

> *"A time of trouble such as has never been seen"* (Daniel 12:1)[8]

Apparently the war of Gog and Magog is not a single event:

---

[7] A potential exists for a major war against the Jewish people at the end of history as the threshold to *Yemos HaMoshiach*.

[8] Other references include *Zechariah* (12-14), *Yirmiyahu* (30), *Daniel* (11-12), *Yoel* (4), and *Tehillim* (83). It is also referred to in the Talmud, for example: *Shabbos* 118a and *Avodah Zarah* 3b.

After *Moshiach* comes, a major war will be insti-
gated against Israel, as mentioned in the Holy
Zohar (*Shemos* 7b), and in *Parashas Vayaira*
(119a) and *Toldos* (139). This is the war of Gog
and Magog spoken about in *Yechezkel* (38, 39),
and *Zechariah* (14), as well as in *Midrash
Tehillim* (*Mizmor* 118:9). There it says: *Three*
times in the future Gog and Magog will come
against Israel and go up against Jerusalem, and
assemble and anger the nations with him to go
up to Jerusalem... (*Sha'arei Leshem*, p. 491)

Hence, there are meant to be three separate
wars of Gog and Magog, and according to the following, two have already occurred:

"While in London I heard from the holy Rabbi
Elchanan Wasserman, quoting the Chofetz
Chaim, that *Chazal* say the war of Gog and Magog will be threefold. After the First World War,
the Chofetz Chaim said that it was the first battle
of Gog and Magog, and that in about twenty-five
years[9] there would be a second world war, which
would make the first one seem insignificant.
Then there would be a third battle... (*Leiv
Eliyahu, Shemos*, p. 172)

---

[9] About 1942.

Thus, the race for time. *Moshiach* has not yet come, or at least, he has yet to reveal himself to the world.[10] According to the Holy *Zohar*, *Techiyas HaMeisim* is meant to begin in 27 years time, and *Kibbutz Golios* may have already begun in 1990. And, we live 13 years into a period of history that corresponds to the hour during which Adam *HaRishon* ate from the forbidden Tree of Knowledge of Good and Evil on the sixth day of Creation.

In the meantime, FOUR-FIFTHS—*at least*—of the Jewish people has yet to return to the fold, and show very little, if any, movement in that direction. The State of Israel remains intensely secular, the government confused, and the people torn. The Orthodox world, for that matter, is not faring well enough, at least not enough to counter-balance all the negative

---

[10] Before *Moshiach Ben Dovid will come*, there will be *Moshiach Ben Yosef,* referred to in many places, such as *Succah* 52a and 52b in the Talmud. *Kol HaTor* is devoted to discussing his role in the redemption process, which is quite extensive. And, even though it is said that he will die in battle, according to some opinions it all depends upon how much of his work we do in advance of his appearance, such as ingathering exiles to Israel and revealing *Sod* to the Jewish people (*Ramchal* on the *Idra* of Rebi Shimon bar Yochai, *Moshiach Ben Yosef*). According to the Vilna Gaon, this is the *sod* of the words, *"Yosef is still alive"* (*Bereishis* 45:26): the decree to die at the hands of Armelius does not have to be fulfilled (*Kol HaTor*, Chapter 1:6a, q.v. *Od Yosef Chai*).

influences in the world today.

And yet, one more war of Gog and Magog remains unaccounted for—as anti-Semitism gets worse with each passing day, and the entire world angrily moves in on Jerusalem and the Jewish people. History certainly seems to be building towards some kind of ultimate climax.

As *b'ittah* approaches, the chance for *achishenah* fades.

However, the truth is, we have already been in transition for some time now, and for all we know, *Yemos HaMoshiach* has already begun. Indeed, if Rava's words are true—and we have presented evidence in their favor throughout—then we can expect very strong parallels between the redemption from Egypt and the Final Redemption.

The redemption of the Jewish people from Egyptian servitude had been spectacular. From the moment that Moshe first appeared before Pharaoh and turned his staff into a snake, to the death of the Egyptian firstborn one year later, it had been all one long process of redemption.

Well, *not exactly*. In fact, in spite of Moshe's demonstration in Pharaoh's palace, the Jewish people did not go free. And, not only did they not go free, but Pharaoh increased their slavery, forcing a dejected Moshe to return to God and complain:

God, why have You done evil to this people, why have You sent me? From the time that I came to Pharaoh to speak in Your Name he did evil to this people, but You did not rescue Your people." (*Shemos* 5:22-23)

However, God reprimanded Moshe by telling him:

"Now you will see what I shall do to Pharaoh, for through a strong hand will he send them out, and with a strong hand will he drive them from his land." (*Shemos* 6:1)

In other words, God told Moshe, what you perceive as prolonged slavery is, in fact, the beginning of the redemption. Yes, your request on My behalf resulted in Pharaoh's increasing the burden on the Children of Israel. However, it was a necessary first step in the direction of their redemption, and in time you will understand why.

If Moshe was a hard sell about the impending redemption, then the enslaved and embittered Jewish people still back in Egypt were even more difficult to convince. Indeed, when Moshe *Rabbeinu* returned the second time to tell them that soon they would go free, the Torah reports:

Moshe told it to the Children of Israel, but they did not listen to Moshe because their spirit was broken, and because of the hardness of their work. (Shemos 6:9)

When the Ten Plagues finally did begin 12 months in advance of the exodus,[11] and Egypt was finally made to suffer somewhat, hope was rekindled for some Jews. Nevertheless, they still remained slaves to Pharaoh for the time being, and would remain so until Rosh Hashanah of the upcoming year—7 months later.[12]

From *that* point onward the Jewish people stopped working while Egypt was being systematically destroyed. For the *one-fifth* of the total Jewish population that believed the redemption was at hand, it was just a matter of sitting back and biding their time until God finally opened the door to redemption all the way.[13]

In the meantime, what had Jewish life been like?

---

[11] Nisan 2447; *Seder Olam*, Chapter 3.

[12] *Sha'arei Leshem*, page 408.

[13] As *Rashi* quotes from the *Mechilta*, only *one-fifth* of the Jews left Egypt with Moshe *Rabbeinu*, the other *four-fifths* having died in the Plague of Darkness (*Rashi, Shemos* 13:18). Apparently, the other four-fifths did not wait for the redemption to come, in spite of the miracles taking place around them in their favor.

The miracles had been so great at the time that even Pharaoh's magicians had been compelled to admit that God was their Source.[14] Surely, then, life for the Jew had become supernatural as well, ending any need to take care of everyday mundane matters.

Not really:

> At the beginning of the redemption there were great miracles and yet, the Jewish people remained quite physical and material . . . the redemption being a function of both great miracles and nature. (*Sha'arei Leshem,* p. 488)

Thus, for part of the period of redemption, two realities co-existed, that of miracle and of nature. While the plagues miraculously obliterated Egypt, the Jewish people were still required to take care of everyday matters in a very natural manner:

> The *zuhama* was not removed from them until the giving of Torah. (*Sha'arei Leshem,* p. 488)

That is, the spiritual impurity from the Original Snake in *Gan Aiden* was not removed from the Jewish people until they accepted Torah at *Har Sinai* (*Shabbos* 146a), a necessary stage for rising above nature.

---

[14] *Shemos* 8:15.

Once that happened, then the everyday reality of the Jewish people became completely supernatural, until they sinned with the golden calf.[15]

Even after that, we are told:

Your clothing did not wear out, nor did your feet suffer throughout these forty years. (Devarim 8:4)

Not to mention that the *manna* was absorbed by every limb of the body, eliminating the need for issues of personal hygiene as well.[16]

However, until that time, it was miracle and nature working together.[17] Likewise will it be in the Days of *Moshiach:*

It will be the same way in *Yemos HaMoshiach*, with the redemption being a function of both great miracles and nature; the entire world will remain quite physical, as well as the Jewish people. Any annulment of *zuhama* and refinement

---

[15] *Sha'arei Leshem*, page 453. This was symbolized by the letters flying back to Heaven from the first set of *Luchos* with which Moshe descended, just before he broke them (*Pesachim* 87b; *Pirkei d'Rebi Eliezer,* Chapter 45).

[16] *Yoma* 75b.

[17] Perhaps, this is why so many Jews still found in possible to doubt the upcoming redemption.

of physicality will only begin later, and it will progress slowly, for this is a major transition, as it says: One *verse* says, *"Who magnifies—magdil— the victories of His king"* (*Tehillim* 18:51), yet another *verse* says, *"He is a tower —migdol—of His king's salvations"* (II *Shmuel* 22:51). Rebi Yudan says: It is because the redemption for this people will not come suddenly, but will progress over time. What does "magnify" —*magdil*— mean? It will become increasingly larger—*mis-gadeles*—and continue…For this reason, the redemption is compared to the dawn, as it says, *"Then your light will burst out like the dawn"* (*Yeshayahu* 58:8) (*Midrash Shochar Tov, Mizmor 19*). (Ibid.)

This is *very* important to know, not just because it allows us to gain a deeper appreciation of what the Jews in Egypt underwent, but because of what the Jews of *Moshiach's* time will undergo.

Therefore, *Yemos HaMoshiach* could have already begun and we wouldn't necessarily even know it. On the contrary, just as in Egypt the Jewish situation seemed to be getting worse at the beginning of the redemption, so too in *Moshiach's* time will it appear to get worse as the redemption gets underway. It will take time before the Final Redemption becomes obvious to *all*.

According to the Vilna Gaon, the light of *Moshiach* became earthbound a *LONG* time ago:

> [The Vilna Gaon] was born in the year 480[18] (1720 CE), and he saw in this the sign to which the following *verse* alludes: *"And Miriam took the drum (tav-peh) in her hand"* (*Shemos* 16:20); [she took it] against the *Sitra Achra* (for, the *gematria* of *"tav-peh"* and one of the names of the *Sitra Achra* are both 480). The mission of the [Vilna Gaon to be *Moshiach Ben Yosef*] is hinted to in the [words from the] *verse,* *"perfect stone"*[19] (*Devarim* 25:15) in *Parashas Ki Seitzei.* In other words, in the sixth century, our rabbi reached the [level of the] light of *Moshiach Ben Yosef* when he became 20 years old in the year [5]500. Hence, the "last generation" began from the first "hour" of the light of "morning" of the sixth millennium, at which time he merited the revelation of Ya'akov *Avinu*; the greatest mysteries of the entire period of *Moshiach* were revealed to him until the time of great wonders, including the end of days. (*Kol HaTor,* Chapter

---

[18] That is, 5480, but in Hebrew dating the millennium is often left out since it only changes once every 1000 years.

[19] In Hebrew, *"evven shlaimah"*, which the *GR"A* understood to be a hint to his name, "E(liyahu) ben Shlomo".

3:8)[20]

The *Gaon's* mastery of Kabbalah, and all aspects of Torah for that matter, is legendary, as was his expertise in secular matters as well. This itself was a sign of his great potential to be *Moshiach Ben Yosef,* for one of the main roles of *Moshiach Ben Yosef* is to reveal the secrets of Torah:

> At the beginning of the redemption, that is, *"the time to favor her"* (*Tehillim* 102:14), which is through the Beginning-*Moshiach*,[21] mysteries of the Torah and of *Chazal* will begin to be revealed. As a result, there will be understanding of the "beginning" and the "footprints" of *Moshiach*...[The *Gaon*] was permitted by Heaven to reveal secrets of the Torah regarding the footprints of *Moshiach, b'sod "Tzafnas Pa'-*

---

[20] As mentioned in Chapter 3, each millennium corresponds to one day of creation. According to most commentators each day of Creation was 24 hours long, but we look at them as 12-hour days when calculating the proportion of a one-hour period within a millennium, since God did not do any creating at night (*Sha'arei Leshem*, page 289). However, the *GR"A* is dealing with a 24-hour long day in this comparison to the sixth millennium,.

[21] That is, *Moshiach Ben Yosef* who precipitates the Final Redemption.

nayach,"[22] and to teach us about the events of the period of the "Footprints of *Moshiach*" according to their words. (*Kol HaTor*, Chapter 1:12)

This would certainly help to explain why, around that time, Kabbalah became more *revealed*. It was during the lifetime of Rabbi Yitzchak Luria (1534-1572 BCE)—the *Arizal*—that *Toras Nistar* exploded into the public realm, and the *Zohar* itself provides an explanation why:

The men of understanding will know, because they are from the side of [the eighth *sefirah* called] *Binah*, which is the "Tree of Life." Of them it says, *"The Maskilim will emanate light like the light of the sky" (Daniel* 12:3)...with this work of yours, *Sefer HaZohar,* which is from the light of *Binah*, which is called *"teshuvah."*[23] In the future *Yisroel* will taste from the "Tree of Life," which is this *Sefer HaZohar*, and they will leave exile in mercy, and, *"God alone will lead them, and they will have no foreign god" (De-*

---

[22] This was the name Pharaoh gave to Yosef, which means "Revealer of Hidden Matters" (*Bereishis* 41:45).

[23] The understanding necessary for *teshuvah* is said to come from *Binah*.

varim 32:12). (*Zohar* 124b)

—once more making the point that *Sod* is crucial for a merciful redemption.

The *Arizal* taught:

> For these ten colleagues,[24] all the secrets of Torah were revealed and explained without any suffering. This will not occur again until the Generation of *Moshiach*, as mentioned in the *Zohar* in many places. (*Sha'ar HaGilgulim*, Introduction 39)

—something that seems to be occurring more and more with each passing day.

Thus, events are occurring—*and have been occurring for some time now*—that strongly suggest, according to the great Torah leaders and Kabbalists of the past, that the Final Redemption is well in swing. Indeed, only to the untrained eye do the events we are witnessing today seem only partially significant, having little to do with an incipient redemption process.

Based upon all that has been presented and analyzed, the question is not, *"Are we in transition?"* but rather,

---

[24] The students of Rebi Shimon bar Yochai.

"At what stage of transition are we?"[25]

Miracles abound, though we may take them for granted, especially since many of them are negative, such as increased anti-Semitism.[26] Nature also abounds, which only makes matters more confusing for so many Jews around the world, as it did for the four-fifths who died in Egypt.

And, there is resistance to *Kibbutz Golios* from all sides of the Jewish and non-Jewish world. However, as the *GR"A* warned:

> According to our teacher, as the measure of *Kibbutz Golios* increases so will the strength of the *Sitra Achra*, and opposers will increase against those who are not devoted to carrying out the ingathering. Then there will be refuge in *Tzion* and *Yerushalayim,* and there will be survivors.

---

[25] The Talmud lists signs that one can expect to see during the end of days, and many, if not all of them, seem to have occurred (*Sanhedrin* 97a).

[26] As the Talmud says, anti-Semitism is always supernatural (*Shabbos* 89a). As the *Maharal* explains: Israel's unique quality is Divine and supernatural, and such a quality cannot co-exist with any defect. And, since this quality is intrinsic to Israel, when they lack it [it is as if] they cease to exist. Therefore, when Israel does not do God's will...by rights they ought to be completely annihilated, but instead they are delivered into the power of a lowly nation (*Chidushei Aggaddos*, 1, page 153).

Regarding this, our teacher was very concerned. (*Kol HaTor*, Chapter 1:10)

However, as is the case with all such resistance, it is in order to test Jewish resolve, to allow us to make free-will decisions and to earn the appropriate reward for doing so. Unfortunately, it is also such resistance that distracts many from understanding what is truly transpiring: *transition to Yemos HaMoshiach*.

Yemos HaMoshiach

thirteen

JUST TO REITERATE, *Yemos HaMoshiach*—Days of *Moshiach*—is a period of time that bridges between *Olam HaZeh*—This World—and *Techiyas HaMeisim*—Resurrection of the Dead. The former period began with the creation of man,[1] and the latter period, according to the *Zohar HaKodesh*, will begin no later than the Jewish year 5790, or 2030 CE.[2]

---

[1] Even though man was not created until Day Six of creation, that is considered to be the official starting point of human history. Hence, Rosh Hashanah, which falls on the first day of Tishrei and originally was on Day Six, is considered to be the "birthday" of creation, even though the actual first day was five days earlier on the 25th of Elul.

[2] This was discussed already in Chapter Four.

Proportionally, it is a very small period of time. *Olam HaZeh* is now 5763 years old, and *Techiyas HaMeisim* will be at least 210 years long. That leaves only 27 years (at the time of this writing) for *Yemos HaMoshiach*, and the period becomes shorter with each passing day that *Moshiach* does not arrive. However, as mentioned in the previous essay, for all we know, *Yemos HaMoshiach* may already have begun.

In fact, when the Talmud writes:

> There is no difference between This World and *Yemos HaMoshiach* except for the oppression of nations. (*Brochos* 34b)

it may be talking about the part of *Yemos HaMoshiach* we may presently be living in, as the following discusses:

> Nature and physicality will remain until the time of *Techiyas HaMeisim*, which will begin no less than forty years after the "Ingathering of the Exiles," as it says in *Midrash Ne'elam*[3] (*Toldos* 139a,140a; *Shemos* 10a). Regarding that time, it says: "There is no difference between This World and *Yemos HaMoshiach* except for the oppression of nations" (*Brochos* 34b). The world will

_____

[3] Part of the *Zohar*; literally, "Hidden Midrash."

not begin to change from its present, natural state of *zuhama*[4] and physicality until *Techiyas HaMeisim*, and even then, it will happen over time. (*Sha'arei Leshem*, p. 488)

Today, we look at major events as just more insignificant occurrences in the course of 5763 years of history. After *Moshiach* comes and the following is fulfilled:

After, The Holy One, Blessed is He, will take His revenge against them,[5] as spoken about in *Yechezkel*, and the Jewish people will dwell in their land in security and prosperity. *Da'as* (Torah knowledge) will greatly increase, as will wisdom and purity... (*Sha'arei Leshem,* p. 491)

we will look at the same events through the prism of *Yemos HaMoshiach*, and see *then* how they were very much a part of this period.

However, as small and as close a period of time it may be, do we know anything about it? What will life be like after *Moshiach* has rid the world of evil?

To begin with, the Talmud says:

---

[4] Spiritual impurity from the Original Snake.

[5] Gog and Magog, and the nations they will rally against Israel.

Rebi Yehudah elucidated: In the Time-to-Come, The Holy One, Blessed is He, will bring the *yetzer hara* and slaughter it before the righteous and before the evil... (*Succah* 52a)

Thus, one of the first major changes that will occur is the destruction of the *yetzer hara*, man's evil inclination. How else could the oppression of nations cease, as the Talmud says, if the very source of all man's negative traits is not first eliminated? Finally, good will triumph over evil, and *forever*.

The downside of this is that, with the elimination of the *yetzer hara*, free-will will also become a thing of the past:

The Holy One, Blessed is He, gave a portion of His glory to flesh-and-blood, to make him a partner with Him in Creation...And, just as The Holy One, Blessed is He, created everything according to His will and without being compelled, God forbid, likewise He gave this possibility to man as well, by allowing him to act and perform according to his own will. This was accomplished through the creation of good and evil, for had The Holy One, Blessed be He, created only good, man would be compelled to act [in a good way only], and there would be no purpose for any of the abilities that were given to him...

(*Sha'arei Leshem*, p. 76)

The *Ramchal* adds:

As we have discussed, man is the creature created for the purpose of being drawn close to God.
He is placed between perfection and deficiency,
with the power to earn perfection. Man must
earn this perfection, however, through his own
free will and desire. If he were compelled to
choose perfection, then he would not actually
be its master, and God's purpose would not be
fulfilled. It was therefore necessary that man be
created with free will. Man's inclinations are
therefore balanced between good and evil,[6] and
he is not compelled toward either of them. He
has the power of choice, and is able to choose
either side, knowingly and willingly, as well as to
possess whichever one he wishes. Man was
therefore created with both a Good Urge—*Yetzer Tov*—and an Evil Urge—*Yetzer Hara*. He has
the power to incline himself in whichever direc-

---

[6] As the *Ramchal* explains shortly, the perfect balance ended
after Adam ate from the Tree of Knowledge of Good and Evil,
and as a result, *"the heart of man is evil from his youth"*
(*Bereishis* 8:21). Thus, the power of free-will was limited, re-
quiring the help of God to overcome the tendencies of the
yetzer hara (*Kiddushin* 30b).

tion he desires. (*Derech Hashem*, 1:3:1)

Therefore, remove the evil inclination from Creation and good becomes an automatic reality. In fact, this had been attempted once before, at least in part, by the rabbis of the Talmud with the following results:

"Then Yehoshua stood upon the platform of the Levi'im, with Bani, Kadmiel, Shebaniah, Bunni, Sherebiah, Bani, and Chenani, and they cried out in a loud voice to God" (Nechemiah 9:4). What did they say? Rav Yehudah, and according to others, Rebi Yochanan said, they cried, "Woe, woe, it is this (the *yetzer hara*) that destroyed the Temple, burnt the *Heichal*, killed all the just men, and exiled Israel from their land, and still it dances among us! Why did You give it to us? Is it not in order to give us greater reward for overcoming it? However, we want neither it nor the great rewards"...They fasted three days and three nights, and then it (the evil inclination) was delivered into their hands. The result was that a flame in the shape of a young lion came out of the Holy of Holies. "Here he is, the evil inclination of idolatry," the prophet called to Israel, as it is says, *"This is the evil"* (Zechariah 5:8). While they were catching him, a hair was torn out of his mane; he issued a cry which was

heard for a distance of four hundred miles. They said: "If he cries so loudly, what can we do to him? What can we do so that his voice be not heard so that Heaven should not pity him?" They were advised by the prophet to throw him into a leaden boiler, as lead absorbs sound. They put him into a leaden boiler and covered it with a leaden lid, as it is says, *"This is the evil"* (*Zechariah* 5:8). So he threw it into the midst of the *ephah* and he put the heavy lead cover over its opening. They then said: "Since it is a favorable moment, let us pray against sensual desire." So they prayed, and it was delivered to them. The prophet told them, "Be careful, if you kill this spirit, the entire world will be destroyed." They kept him imprisoned for three days. After, they looked for an egg laid on that day for a sick person, but it could not be found in all of *Eretz Yisroel*.[7] They said among themselves: "What should we do? If we kill him, the world will be destroyed. Should we pray for part? There is a tradition that things are not given in halves from Heaven." So they blinded him in both of his eyes and left him, and as a result, since then he does

---

[7] Without the *yetzer hara* in the world, the drive to procreate was removed from creation.

not arouse desire towards relatives.[8] (*Yoma* 69b)

The prophet describes *Yemos HaMoshiach* as follows:

"I will sanctify My Great Name . . . And I will take you from the nations and gather you… And I will sprinkle pure waters upon you… And I will give you a new heart and a new spirit…I will put My spirit within you, and I will make it so that you will follow My decrees and keep My judgments and do them. You will dwell in the land…" (*Yechezkel* 36:23-28)

"[Israel] will no longer be divided…They will no longer be contaminated…My servant Dovid will be king over them, and there will be one shepherd for all of them; they will follow My judgments and keep My decrees and follow them. They will dwell on the land…" (*Yechezkel* 37:22-25)

This is the power of removing the *yetzer hara* from man. All of mankind's misgivings and faulty perspectives that lead him to make incorrect decisions about himself, the world around him, and his purpose

---

[8] The drive for incest ended, or was at least greatly reduced.

in life stem from his *yetzer hara*. Without the *yetzer hara*, all that man has been told and knows to be good automatically becomes his reality, including the *mitzvos*.[9]

Thus, the *gematria* of "*nachash*" (snake; 50+8+300) equals that of "*Moshiach*" (40+300+10+8), to indicate that it is only the *yetzer hara*, which was embodied in the Original Snake, that stands between this world and utopia.[10]

If this is the case, that free-will is finished forever and therefore, our chance to increase our portions in the World-to-Come, then what will be the point of *Yemos HaMoshiach?* This:

> Resurrection itself won't happen all at once, as it says: In the future, *tzaddikim* will resurrect the dead (*Pesachim* 68a).[11] Before the resurrection, *zuhama* will be eliminated and physicality of the body will decompose, as it is taught: In the future, *tzaddikim* will be dust, for it says, "*Until you return to the earth from where you were taken. You are dust, and to dust you will return*" (*Bereishis* 3:19), (*Shabbos* 152b). When

---

[9] *Sha'arei Leshem*, page 488.

[10] *Pri Tzaddik, Chukas* 16.

[11] Implying that *tzaddikim* will have already resurrected whereas other less righteous people will have yet to.

does this occur? Moments before *Techiyas HaMeisim*, when all those still living will die to allow for the physicality of the body to decompose and be transformed from *"Kesones Ohr"* (AYIN-Vav-Raish) to *"Kesones Ohr"* (ALEPH-Vav-Raish).[12] Death, at that time, will no longer be the result of the Angel of Death, *God forbid*, for by that time he will have been eliminated completely, as it says: In the Time-to-Come, The Holy One, Blessed is He, will bring the *yetzer hara* and slaughter it before the righteous and before the evil (*Succah* 52a). At that time, since the world will be completely purified from *zuhama*, death will come *directly* from The Holy One, Blessed is He, Himself, for the sake of immediate resurrection with a new body like that of Adam *HaRishon* before the sin, as when he entered *Gan Aiden*. It is to this that the *Midrash Ne'elam* (*Vayaira* 113b) refers when it quotes, "*I*

---

[12] The first term means "Clothing of Skin," and the second term means "Clothing of Light." Before Adam *HaRishon* ate from the Tree of Knowledge of Good and Evil, his skin was translucent like a fingernail is. However, as a result of the sin, creation was transformed and became more physical, and man's skin of light became the opaque physical skin that now encompasses our entire body. This process will be reversed in *Techiyas HaMeisim*, but it will begin somewhat already in *Yemos HaMoshiach*.

bring death and I give life" (Devarim 32:39).
For, death at that time will be *directly* from The
Holy One, Blessed is He, only, as was the case
with Moshe *Rabbeinu's* death, and that of the
Forefathers, Aharon and Miriam (*Bava Basra*
17a). This is also spoken about elsewhere in the
Zohar: With respect to that time, it is written,
*"See now that it is I, I am Him, and there is no
god with Me; I will bring death and I give life."*
Until that time death was the result of the *Sitra
Achra*,[13] but, from that time onward, no one will
taste death. Rather, it will be from The Holy One,
Blessed is He, Who will bring death to us and
resurrect us immediately. Why? Since *zuhama*
will no longer exist, and it will be a new world,
loyal to The Holy One, Blessed is He. (*Zohar,
Mishpatim* 108b). (*Sha'arei Leshem*, p. 488)

Thus, another one of the major transformations
in the time of *Moshiach* will not be an absence of
death, but the way in which it will occur. As the Talmud says, there are 903 forms of death, and
"*neshikah*"—Divine Kiss—is the most pleasant of all.[14]
It was the way in which people like the Forefathers
and Moshe *Rabbeinu* were taken from this world,

---

[13] The "Obstructing Angel," also known as the "Angel of Death."
[14] *Brochos* 8a.

brought about by an encounter with the Divine Presence that is too sublime for the body to survive.

Another difference has to do with Torah itself.

We know from the Torah that Moshe *Rabbeinu* first descended with a set of tablets that had been carved out by God and engraved by God.[15] However, as a result of the incident of the golden calf, Moshe broke that set of *luchos* and was forced to return to Heaven for a second set.

However, the second set of *luchos* was different from the first ones, this time being carved by man—Moshe himself[16]—though God had again engraved them. And, this difference was anything but small, for it represented the great difference in the spiritual level of the Jewish people as a result of the sin of the golden calf, compared to what they achieved upon accepting the Torah months earlier. It also represented the fundamental difference in the appearance of Torah as we have it now, compared to how it will appear in *Yemos HaMoshiach*.

In Kabbalistic terms, the first set of tablets was on the level of *"Toras Atzilus,"* whereas the second set is on the level of what is called, *"Toras Beriyah."* The difference between the two is basically the difference between *Sod* and the rest of the levels of Torah, as de-

---

[15] *Shemos* 32:16.
[16] *Shemos* 34:1.

scribed below:

> The main rectification (*tikun*) from learning Kabbalah more than any other part of Torah learning is that the rest of the areas[17] are clothed in matters of this world, which is not the case with Kabbalah, and particularly the words of the *Arizal*, who built upon the *"Ideres"* and *"Sifra d'Tzniusa,"*[18] and the other secret sections of the Holy *Zohar*. All of its matters deal only on the level of *"Atzilus"* and the worlds of the light of *"Ain Sof."* That is why the wisdom of Kabbalah is called *"Nistar"*—Hidden. (*Drushei Olam Ha-Tohu*, 1:5:7:8)

If this sounds complicated and abstract, that is because it is. Underlying this short paragraph is a world of Kabbalistic fundamentals and explanations that would require volumes to make clear. However, the main point can be explained in far fewer words.

We have already discussed the concept of *Pardes* and the four levels of Torah learning to which they allude: *Pshat, Remez, Drush,* and *Sod*. However, these four levels represent far more than just rungs on an

---

[17] The Written Law, Mishnah, Talmud, etc..

[18] Two of the most Kabbalistic and technical sections of the *Zohar*.

intellectual ladder—they represent four planes of spiritual consciousness. They are, from top to bottom: *Atzilus, Beriyah, Yetzirah, Asiyah.* [19]

These four levels also correspond to nine[20] of the Ten *Sefiros*, the system of spiritual filters that God created to make His light safely accessible to man, and four of the five levels of the human soul, as follows:

Pardes	Sefirah	World	Soul Level
	Keser	A. Kad.	Yechidah
Sod	Chochmah	Atzilus	Chayah
Drush	Binah	Beriyah	Neshamah
Remez	Chesed-Yesod	Yetzirah	Ruach
Pshat	Malchus	Asiyah	Nefesh

Thus, the intellectual journey from *Pshat* to *Sod* is also a spiritual journey from *Asiyah* to *Atzilus*, and from *Nefesh* to *Chayah*. This is why when someone learns Torah with *complete sincerity*, and after acquiring[21] a specific level of Torah he enters a higher realm, he *automatically* becomes more righteous and therefore closer to God.

----

[19] See Chapter 6.

[20] There level above *Atzilus* is too sublime to discuss in these terms and corresponds to the *Keser*.

[21] This means means making the concepts part of one's personal psyche.

However, the Kabbalists do not only refer to this system as ascending levels, but they also view it as a series of concentric circles, like the many layers of skin on an onion; the more sublime the level, the more internal it is. Thus, *Sod-Chochmah-Atzilus-Chayah* would be the innermost of all four layers, and *Pshat-Malchus-Asiyah-Nefesh* would be the outermost layers, enwrapping the other three within it.

Thus, in a sense, *Drush* "clothes" *Sod*, *Remez* clothes both *Drush* and *Sod*, and *Pshat* hides all three. And, therefore, if *Toras Beriyah* refers to the more external three layers of Torah learning, then it clothes *Toras Atzilus*, which corresponds to the level of *Sod*, as we learned above.

How does it actually do this?

Everything in Creation, physical or spiritual, is an expression of an abstract concept, a projection of the Divine will which is sublime and perfect. It exists as it does because God put the original idea into Creation, and subjected it to rules and immutable principles that govern Creation according to His will.

However, as the concept moves from the realm of the abstract to that of the physical, it takes on layers that hide its inner essence. The more physical it becomes, the more layers it requires, and the more hidden the essence of the concept becomes.

For example, the Written Torah is made up of narratives and stories, and some technical details as well. Every letter and crown of Torah teaches us something about Creation and its purpose, but it is easy to overlook this fact once one becomes "distracted" by what is portrayed in the Torah.

However, the Oral Law, specifically the Mishnah, extracts only the technical information from the Written Law, because its prime concern is to teach Jewish law. Even the stories are only a point of focus if they have something *halachic* to teach.

However, the Talmud is interested not just in the technical law of the Mishnah, but the principle behind it, and its expression of Divine will. Very often, it will take the laws of the Mishnah to unlikely extremes, just to get to the bottom of a concept and its role in everyday life.

Kabbalah, on the other hand, is interested in seeing how the actual concept is a building block of God's Creation. *Sod* traces all that exists to its earliest root in the creation process, at least as much as God has permitted us to see. And, in doing this, one comes as close to the purest expression of Divine will that one can, at least while in human form.

This last level of Torah-learning will be the everyday learning of *Yemos HaMoshiach*. It will create a world of difference beyond our present comprehesion. It is this level of Torah knowledge that was embodied in the first set of *luchos.*[22] The Vilna Gaon called it *"Toras Moshiach."*[23]

Thus, if the layers of Torah become more "transparent" during *Yemos HaMoshiach*, then so do the levels of soul. This is why the performance of *mitzvos* becomes second nature at this time, as the following implies:

> In this world, if a man goes to collect figs on Shabbos the figs say nothing! In the future, if a man goes to collect figs on Shabbos the figs will yell out, *"It's Shabbos!"* (*Midrash Shochar Tov, Mizmor 73*)

And, as one would expect, prophecy will return. Since the everyday reality will have become elevated and the world will be rid of the spiritual impositions that separated man from the Divine Presence, prophecy will also be an everyday occurrence. Not just prophecy, but the ability to communicate with others

---

[22] The intellectual gap between each of the four levels is not equidistant. The difference in depth of understanding between *Pshat* and *Remez*—Torah and *Mishnah*—is less than the difference between *Remez* and *Drush*—*Mishnah* and Talmud. However, the difference between the level of *Drush* and *Sod* is far greater than the difference in levels of understanding between *Remez* and *Drush* (*Sha'ar HaGilgulim*, Introduction 16).

[23] *Kol HaTor* 5:2:7.

without the need for physical speech, for like most of the organs in the human body, mouths and ears were given physical expression as a result of the intermingling of good and evil when Adam *HaRishon* ate from the Tree of Knowledge of Good and Evil.[24]

What is the purpose of the heart? What is the purpose of the liver, or the kidneys, etc.? They act as *filters*, as systems to separate good from bad, in order to utilize the good and reject the bad, something that became necessary to do once Adam caused good and evil to intermingle through his sin. This process of separation is called "*Birrur*."[25]

However, without free-will, there will no longer be any need for *birrur*. Since evil will be completely eliminated, the world will become perfectly good, like the *manna* the Jewish people ate for forty years in the desert, which did not require any type of filtering.

Thus, as the Talmud points out, there will also be little need for most of the processes that man has to implement *now* just to stay alive:

> Rebi Chiya bar Yosef said: The Land of Israel is destined to yield ready-made cakes and ready-made cloaks…The wheat will sprout and rise

---

[24] *Sha'arei Leshem*, page 344.

[25] Thus *Borrer* is one of the 39 creative activities forbidden on Shabbos.

like palms on mountain tops, and if one will think that it will be difficult to harvest it...The Holy One, Blessed is He, will cause a wind to be brought from His treasures which will blow upon it and make its flower fall off. Then man will go out into the field and bring handfuls of corn from which he will support himself and his family. (*Kesuvos* 111b)

In fact, as time moves on in this idyllic spiritual environment, all that occurs will only be for the purpose of uplifting the body and preparing it for its final rectification in *Techiyas HaMeisim*. Physicality will remain until the very end of this period of time, though according to the Midrash those who made *aliyah* prior to *Moshiach's* arrival will start the process of reverting back to "*Kesones Ohr*"—with the *aleph*—even during this time.

This has been a brief description of this period of time that is meant to act as the threshold to the next one—*Techiyas HaMeisim*.

Techiyas HaMeisim

fourteen

WHAT DO WE mean by the *"End of Days"?* Usually, the expression refers only to the period of time just in *advance* of and including the arrival of *Moshiach*, in which case we could have ended this book two chapters ago. However, here we will use the term to refer to the end of *all* the days, that is, all the days up until the year 6000.

After that begins the seventh millennium, the period of time referred to by the rabbis as, *"yom sh'kulo Shabbos"* "the day that is completely Shabbos."

When a soul leaves its body, it enters this Soul World and remains there in a state of rest while the body undergoes what it must. During this period, the soul experiences sublime delight, very much like that which will be bestowed on the individual later in the period of genuine reward. Its level in the Soul World is also determined by its accomplishments, just as is the ultimate reward. The true perfection destined for those worthy of it, however, is not attained by either the body or soul alone, but by both of them combined after the resurrection.[1] (*Derech Hashem* 1:3:11)

At the end of this 1000 years,[2] the body and soul are once again brought back together, to be judged as a single unit, as the Talmud teaches:

Antoninus said to Rebi, "The body and the soul may excuse themselves from judgment. How so? The body can say, 'The soul sinned, for since it

---

[1] Not the period of resurrection of the last 210 years of history, but the period of time that begins at 7000, when body and soul are rejoined again for the final judgment in preparation for the World-to-Come, as the upcoming quote teaches.

[2] "Years" is a borrowed term, since after Year 6000, time, as we have known it, will become irrelevant. We are really referring to periods of time equal to the Divinely-designated time for particular *sefiros* to dominate its corresponding period of history. Between creation and 6000, each *sefirah* that dominated a period of time, *Chesed* through *Yesod*, happened to do so for 1000 years each.

has departed I lie in the grave like a stone.' The soul can say, 'The body sinned, for since I departed from it I fly in the air like a bird.'"

[Rebi] answered him, "I will give you a parable. It is like a king who had an excellent orchard which contained choice figs, over which he appointed two watchmen, one of whom was blind, and the other had no feet. He who had no feet said to the one who was blind, 'I see fine figs in the garden. Place me upon your shoulders, and I shall get them, and we shall eat them.' He did so, and while upon his shoulders he picked the figs, and both ate them. When the owner of the garden came and asked them, 'What happened to my choice figs?' the blind one answered, *'Do I have eyes to see them?'* The lame one answered, *'Have I feet to get them?'* What did the owner do to them? He put the lame one on the shoulders of the blind one and punished them together. So also will The Holy One, Blessed is He, put the soul in the body and punish them together, as it says, *'He will call to the heavens above, and to the earth beneath, to judge His people'* (*Tehillim* 50:4); 'to the heavens above' refers to the soul, and 'to the earth beneath,' refers to the body." (*Sanhedrin* 91a)

Then begins the ultimate period of history, the

one for which it all was created: *Olam HaBah*—the World-to-Come.

Rebi Chiya bar Abba said in the name of Rebi Yochanan, "The glorious future of which all the prophets prophesied is only for him who marries his daughter to a *talmid chacham*, for him who does business with a *talmid chacham*, and for him who gives of his wealth to a *talmid chacham*. But, as for the scholars themselves, *'No eye has witnessed, God, besides You!'* (*Yeshayahu* 64:3). Happy is he who waits for it." What is meant by "No eye has witnessed?" Rebi Yehoshua ben Levi said, "This refers to the wine preserved in its grapes since the six days of Creation." Rebi Shmuel bar Nachmeini said, "This refers to *Aiden* which no eye ever saw. And if you will ask, 'Where did Adam, the first man live?' It was only in the garden [of *Aiden*]. And if you say that 'Garden' and '*Aiden*' are the same, it says, *'And a river went out of Aiden to water the garden'* (*Bereishis* 2:10), [which shows that] 'Garden' and '*Aiden*' are two distinct places." (*Brochos* 34b)

Thus, there are no suitable terms with which to

describe the World-to-Come,[3] and on faith, we know it is worth anything we may have suffered in this world. As the *Ramchal* said, it is the most perfect good man is capable of enjoying.

However, though we may not be able to discuss the World-to-Come experientially, Kabbalah does discuss it in terms of the movement of the *Sefiros* back towards God. Thus, there are three stages of *Olam HaBah*, from 7000–8000, corresponding to the *sefirah* of *Binah*, 8000–9000, corresponding to the *sefirah* of *Chochmah*, and from 9000–10,000, corresponding to *Keser*.[4] At that point, *"HaTikun d'Sod Achdus"*—Rectification of the Mystery of Unity—occurs as Creation approaches its final, eternal position.

In any case, all of that is beyond the scope of the average Jew. So much of the focus of those who believe in the concept of a Final Redemption is on *Yemos HaMoshiach*, for the simple reason that we are embedded in the perils of this world. Simply put, *Yemos HaMoshiach*, whatever it represents and for however long it will last will, at the very least, represent the end to suffering. No one (who remains) will ever doubt God again.

---

[3] The *Maharal* says that since the entire Torah is prophecy, and the prophet can only imagine that which he has experienced before, Moshe could not write about the World-to-Come in the Torah (*Gevuros Hashem*).

[4] *Sha'arei Leshem*, page 519.

However, though the Talmud seems to down-play the changes during this period of time, we have already discussed how even the "smallest" changes will be major. Indeed:

> There won't be any waste product in the food, since the physicality of the body will have become purified. Therefore, as a matter of fact, the food of this time will not be like the food we have now, but rather, all the meals during *Yemos HaMoshiach* will be extremely elevated and far better than any physical pleasure of now, since man himself will have become transformed... All of the pleasures of This World are encased in an unpleasant physicality—the taste of meat is inside the meat itself; the taste of wine is inside the grapes, etc.—and therefore, the pleasure can only be sensed through man's body...However, once the pleasure is enjoyed without any encasements, then every aspect of man will delight in the pleasure and gain life force from it. (*Sha'arei Leshem*, p. 499-500)

Therefore, what the Talmud means is that, compared to what comes later, *Yemos HaMoshiach* is just a short passage of time, a *transition* from This World to *Techiyas HaMeisim* when preparation for the World-to-Come really occurs. *Yemos HaMoshiach* may begin to move us in this direction, but it is the period of *Techiyas HaMeisim* that allows us to return to the original state of man, and *beyond* it.

As mentioned previously, the basic consequence of Adam *HaRishon's* sin was the physicalization of his being, and all of Creation, for that matter:

> Immediately Adam descended tremendously from his level, and so did the worlds to where they are now…They became material, and so did Adam and Chava. Their "clothing" transformed from clothing of light (*Aleph-Vav-Raish*) to clothing of skin (*Ayin-Vav-Raish*), the "skin of the snake." (*Sha'arei Leshem*, p. 344-345)

The goal of rectification, therefore, is to return back to clothing of light. That cannot be achieved during *Yemos HaMoshiach*, as it says:

> In the future, the righteous will be dust, as it says, *"The dust will return to the land as it was"* (*Koheles* 12:7), and it says, *"You are from dust and to dust you will return"* (*Bereishis* 3:19); (*Shabbos* 152b). This will occur a moment before *Techiyas HaMeisim*, when those who are still living will die in order to dissolve the physicality of their bodies in order to transform them from clothing of skin to clothing of light. Death

will not be the result of the Angel of Death then, God forbid, for that was destroyed completely (*Succah* 52a)…but by The Holy One, Blessed is He, Himself, in order to recreate them anew completely, like the body of Adam before the sin when he entered *Gan Aiden*. (*Sha'arei Leshem*, p. 489)

How does it work, and when does it start?

The period of death-resurrection for the entire generation will be long, though righteous people who have died previously will be resurrected immediately at the beginning of the period, after the *forty years* of the ingathering of the exiles. This is what it says in the Midrash, "There will be many resurrections, from the first one after the 40 years of *Kibbutz Golios*, to the last one at the end of the period of, according to Rebi Yehudah, 210 years; Rebi Yitzchak says: 214 years…" (*Midrash Ne'elam, Toldos* 140a). (*Sha'arei Leshem*, p. 489)

Thus, there is a period of history called "*Kibbutz Golios*," when the Jewish exiles will finally return to *Eretz Yisroel*, and that will last *forty* years. This, in turn, will be followed by *Techiyas HaMeisim*, which will last anywhere between 210 and 214 years.

Now, one might think that *Techiyas HaMeisim* begins *after* the year 6000. However, since the *Zohar* has it following *Kibbutz Golios*, which must occur before the year 6000, we can safely conclude that *Techiyas HaMeisim* also occurs before and until Year 6000, as the following corroborates:

> Therefore, Shabbos, *Yom HaKippurim*, and Purim, which allude to periods after *Yemos HaMoshiach*, parts of the World-to-Come, and to eternal lights, will still remain [holidays] in order to allow access to their lights and revelations of the future. However, the rest of the holidays allude only to lights of rectification of *Yemos HaMoshiach*, after which begins the period of *Techiyas HaMeisim* [that continues] until the end of the 6000 years. (*Sha'arei Leshem*, p. 492)

Thus, 6000 years less 210 means that *Techiyas HaMeisim* begins at least by the year 5790, or 2030 CE (according to Rebi Yehudah; according to Rebi Yitzchak, by the year 5786, or 2026 CE). *Kibbutz Golios*, therefore, would have begun as early as 1986 or as late as 1990, as we have already mentioned.

So, imagine it is 5790, and *Moshiach* has already long ago come and finished his work. History as we knew it before his arrival is all but a forgotten reality,

like a distant dream that we are not sure even occurred. The time period since *Moshiach* arrived is
winding down, as the final moments come to a close
in preparation for the next great stage of God's master
plan for man: *Techiyas HaMeisim*. What happens
next?

> Righteous people who have died previously will
> be resurrected *immediately* at the beginning of
> the period, after the *forty years* of the ingather-
> ing of the exiles. (*Sha'arei Leshem*, p. 489)

Regarding those who are resurrected immediately, it says:

> In the future, they will say before the righteous,
> *"Holy!"* (*Bava Basra* 75b); for, all those who will
> still remain [in that period] as they were in This
> World, will say *"Holy!"* before the righteous who
> have already arisen. (*Sha'arei Leshem*, p. 490)

In other words, the period of history will com-
bine both those who have already been resurrected,
and those who await resurrection. And, as holy and
pure as the latter group will be, still, they will not
compare to those who have already been re-built
anew. They will look like angels to those remaining
with their non-resurrected bodies, and they will run to

say *"Holy!"* as they would to angels.

And, once a person is finally resurrected, into which body is it?

If it wasn't for the concept of *gilgulim* (reincarnations), *Techiyas HaMeisim* would be straightforward. Each soul would only have had one body in history,[5] and that's the one that would be resurrected. For those from early history, it might take thousands of years before it happens, but when it does, soul and body would reunite like two old friends. So, the question is, which body is it that is resurrected?

> In the *Zohar* (*Chaye Sarah* 126a), it says that the resurrection will literally occur in the body itself. [It also says that it will occur] in the body that suffered with the soul in this world, and did not derive any pleasure from the entire Torah and his good deeds. This will be after it is purified from all its *zuhama* and physicality, as a result of death and decomposition in the ground. (*Sha'arei Leshem*, p. 489)

In other words, according to this, the purest of all the *gilgulim* comes back in *Techiyas HaMeisim*. The body that "had its cake," but did not yet get a chance to "eat it" during its lifetime is the body that

---

[5] And likewise, only one shot at rectification.

comes back to enjoy the fruits of its labors in the period of resurrection. Since it is the body that sacrificed the most for spiritual gain, but enjoyed the least physical reward for doing so, it is the one to reap the benefits of its self-sacrifice from the past.

However, again, it is not so simple, as the *Arizal* explains:

> When a person is born, his *Nefesh* enters him. If he is adequately rectified through his actions, his *Ruach* will enter him at the end of his *thirteenth* year when he becomes a "complete person." His *Neshamah* will enter him only when he completes his *twentieth* year, as it says in the *Zohar* (*Mishpatim* 94b). (*Sha'ar HaGilgulim*, Introduction 2)

This is talking about the ideal situation, during a person's first *gilgul*. However, should a person not progress in this manner, then the following applies—with major ramifications in *Techiyas HaMeisim*:

> If he does not completely rectify his *Ruach*, then the *Neshamah* will not enter him and he will remain with only his *Nefesh* and *Ruach*. Likewise, if he doesn't completely rectify his *Nefesh*, then he will remain with only his *Nefesh*, lacking both his *Ruach* and *Neshamah*. The *Ruach* and

Neshamah will remain in a place known to The Holy One, Blessed is He, and there a place will be prepared for each one. (*Sha'ar HaGilgulim*, Chapter 2)

In other words, until a person is able to receive all parts of his soul, the parts he has yet to receive remain hidden away with God until the person is ready for them. It can and often does take many lifetimes to finally access those higher levels of soul. Depending upon the level of soul a person has "acquired," thus will be his ability to grow spiritually.

Now, if a person does not completely rectify his *Nefesh* the first time and dies, then his *Nefesh* will have to reincarnate, perhaps even many times until it is sufficiently rectified. Even after complete rectification is achieved, a *Ruach* will not enter him since he only achieved *tikun* through a *gilgul*. (*Sha'ar HaGilgulim*, Introduction 2)

A complication. Had it been his first *gilgul*, then he could have received his *Ruach* while still alive in his *original* body. However, this is not the case with subsequent *gilgulim*. Instead:

He will have to die and return in order to receive

the *Ruach*. Furthermore, once the *Ruach* is sufficiently rectified, then he will also have to reincarnate before receiving a *Neshamah*, as was the case with the *Ruach*. (*Sha'ar HaGilgulim*, Introduction 2)

Thus, after he finally does rectify his *Nefesh* and dies, only in the *next* reincarnation will he return with a *Nefesh* and a *Ruach*. Once the *Ruach* is rectified as well, then he will have to die and come back in another *gilgul* with a *Nefesh*, *Ruach*, and *Neshamah*.

If the *Ruach* is not sufficiently rectified, then the *Nefesh* and the *Ruach* will have to come back again, perhaps many times until the *Ruach* is rectified. Once rectification is achieved, then the person will die and his *Nefesh* and *Ruach* will come back with the proper *Neshamah*, until all three are rectified. One this is done, there is no need for any further *gilgulim*: he has become a "complete person." (*Sha'ar HaGilgulim*, Chapter 2)

This last point is important to know, that it can take many lifetimes to rectify even a single level of soul. As we experience firsthand every day, there is so much temptation to pursue the material world, usually at the cost of the spirituality, and so little strength within many to resist. This is what the Torah means when it says:

> *God said, "I will never again curse the land because of mankind, because the inclination of the heart of man is evil from his youth."* (*Bereishis* 8:21)

Thus, the Talmud warns:

> Difficult is the *yetzer hara* that even its Creator called it "evil," as it says, *"Because the inclination of the heart of man is evil from his youth"* (*Bereishis* 8:21). Rav Shimon, the son of Levi said: Every day the *yetzer* of a man strength-ens itself, seeking to kill him. (*Kiddushin* 30b)

The Talmud concludes that if God doesn't help man fend off his *yetzer hara*, it will consume him in an instant. Apparently, it already has for trillions of people throughout the ages. This is why a person must always pray to God for help against his *yetzer hara*.

Thus, if the *Nefesh* became perfected only after living through at least two *gilgulim*, which body comes back in *Techiyas HaMeisim*? And, if it takes even more *gilgulim* to rectify the *Ruach* and *Neshamah*, then what happens to all the previous bodies of that soul?

Writes Rabbi Chaim Vital:

It seems to me that all levels of rectification are really the fulfillment of *mitzvos* which are dependent upon the "limbs" of the *Nefesh*, and that all blemishes result from violating *Negative Mitzvos*. (*Sha'ar HaGilgulim*, Introduction 4)

In other words, Positive *Mitzvos* which require a person to actively do something cause *tikun* to the *Nefesh*, whereas the transgression of Negative *Mitzvos* blemishes the *Nefesh*.

It is well-known that the completion of the entry of the *Nefesh* into the body, that is, the rectification of the *Nefesh*, is only through the performance of *mitzvos*. And, even though sins blemish the *Nefesh*, they do not prevent its sparks from entering. However, there are two other aspects regarding this matter. If, during the first life he only received his *Nefesh* and didn't merit to completely rectify it and he dies, at the time of Resurrection of the Dead only the specific sections that were rectified return. This is because the first body did not complete the *tikun* of all levels of *Nefesh*. (*Sha'ar HaGilgulim*, Introduction 4)

In other words, a particular reincarnation will be resurrected and receive only those sparks that were rectified through it, while the other parts of the *Nefesh* will return to the bodies in which *they* were rectified. Thus, we learn a new principle: souls can subdivide into different bodies during *Techiyas HaMeisim*, and the division is proportional based upon the amount of sparks that were rectified during a particular body's lifetime.

> Therefore, when this *Nefesh* reincarnates into another body to complete its *tikun* and it achieves its *NR"N* (i.e., *Nefesh, Ruach, Neshamah*), then all the parts of the *Nefesh* that were rectified in the second body, together with the *Ruach* and *Neshamah*, belong to the second body at the time of the resurrection. The first body has no portion in the *Ruach* and *Nefesh*, but does have a share in part of the *Nefesh*, according to that which was rectified with it. The rest of the parts belong to the second body. (*Sha'ar HaGilgulim*, Introduction 4)

A remarkable idea. It turns out that, not only do our souls have different sections, but those sections have sections—many of them—all of which are called "Holy Sparks"—*Nitzotzei Kedushah*. And, what is even more remarkable is that they seem to have a certain independence of their own, able to sustain their own bodies in *Techiyas HaMeisim*.

However, Rav Chaim concludes:

> The main source of pleasure in the Time-to-Come, though, is on the level of *Ruach* and *Neshamah*...He (the resurrected body lacking its *Ruach* and *Neshamah*) will be there in the World-to-Come and have some pleasure, but not the main pleasure since it will lack the appropriate levels of soul—*Ruach* and *Neshamah*—to sense and enjoy it. (*Sha'ar HaGilgulim*, Introduction 4)

Now, though we have discussed the concept of resurrection quite matter-of-factly, we do not really understand what it is actually going to be like during this wondrous period of time. The *Arizal* presented far less than he knew and understood, leaving us instead with only small pieces of the *Techiyas HaMeisim* puzzle. Many questions arise, most of which will probably only begin to be answered after *Moshiach* comes and prophecy begins to return.

The whole concept of *gilgulim* is complicated, because the concept of Holy Sparks, the basis of the human soul, and the process of *tikun* is complicated. To better understand what will occur to the body during *Techiyas HaMeisim*, one has to better understand the concept of the soul and its root within the structure of all human souls, as well as its inter-relationship with other souls from its own root.

However, as we mentioned earlier, at some point in the future all of Creation merges into a single, awesome, and sublime unity with the Creator, as much as is humanly possible. Therefore, whatever happens to our bodies during *Techiyas HaMeisim*, it is still only a preliminary stage along the path to the final level of *tikun* when everything will come together.

Before closing, a few more ideas help to paint a little more of the picture of this period:

> When it says that in the future all sacrifices will no longer be necessary except for the *Todah*—Thanksgiving-Offering, and that all holidays will no longer exist except for Purim and *Yom HaKippurim*, it is referring to the time of resurrection, after the forty years of *Kibbutz Golios* until the end of the 214 years. At that time, the righteous and the meritorious will be on a higher level than angels...as mentioned in the *Zohar HaKodesh* (*Toldos*, 141a)...At that time, a great change will occur to the entire world, even to those still in existence from this world, though they remain quite physical. For, now, the world consists of three categories: impure, pure, and holy; even the "pure" of today is still quite

profane, lacking holiness. However, at that time, *everything* will be on the level of pure and holy. It is with respect to this time that they say all the holidays will no longer apply, for all days will have the holiness of the holidays; weekdays will no longer exist. (*Sha'arei Leshem*, page 491)

In other words, on this side of *Techiyas HaMeisim*, the week is divided between six non-holy weekdays, and one holy day of Shabbos. Occasionally, during the course of the year, holidays are celebrated and when they occur on weekdays, they elevate the day to a level of holiness as well.

However, during *Techiyas HaMeisim*, there will still be seven days of the week, but each one itself will be holy. In fact:

It may be that the days divide into appointed times relevant to them: Sunday, which is the level of *Chesed*, would have the holiness of Pesach; Monday would be Rosh Hashanah; Tuesday: Shavuos; Wednesday: Rosh Chodesh, since it is also called "*Moed*," as the Talmud says (*Shavuos* 10a); Thursday: Succos, because, it is also from the side of *Gevuros*, as it says in the Holy *Zohar* (*Emor* 96a; see there, and the emendations of Rabbi Chaim Vital). Thursday corresponds to *Hod*, which is from the side of *Gevuros*. Friday, which is Day Six, would be Shemini Atzeres, because Day Six corresponds to *Yesod*...This is what it means that all holidays will be annulled in the future, for they will divide up among the days of the week, all of which will have the holiness of the holidays...Therefore, the holidays will be annulled, since the entire period will constantly have the holiness of those holidays. Then, the light that the holidays only hint to now will actually be revealed. Hence, just as they say regarding the seventh millennium, that it will be "a day that is completely Shabbos," so too in *Yemos HaMoshiach* from *Techiyas HaMeisim* and onward, will it be a "time that is completely holiday." For, there are six different types of holy light of the holidays: Pesach, Shavuos, Succos, Shemini Atzeres, Rosh Hashanah and Rosh Chodesh—the *sod* of the root of the six days of the week. When, eventually, their essential lights are actually revealed, they will radiate downward continuously, each day with the holy light of the holiday that is relevant to it. Thus, the entire time will be on the level of the holiness of the holidays. (*Sha'arei Leshem*, page 491)

That is not the final word; there is much more to discuss. However, it is sufficient to provide a glimpse of the direction Creation has been moving now for almost 6000 years. Knowing a little about what to expect when history is all said and done should make it a little easier to put into perspective one's spiritual priorities. And *THAT*, really, is what it is all about, *isn't it?*

Achishenah: I will hasten it

Adam HaRishon: First Man

Aggadic: Told, as in the stories of the Talmud

Alillah: Pretext

Ain Sof: Without Limit; the name given to the Light of God

Aitz HaDa'as Tov v'Rah: Tree of Knowledge of Good and Evil

Aliyah: Ascending (to Israel)

Amos: Plural of "*amah*"; a measure of about 2 feet

Arizal: Acronym: Godly Rebi Yitzchak, remember for blessing

Asiyah: Action; lowest of four "worlds"

Atarah: Crown

Atzilus: Emanations; highest of four "worlds"

Avinu: Our father

Ba'al Teshuvah: Master of *Teshuvah*

Beriyah: Creation; second highest "world" after *Atzilus*

B'ezras Hashem: With the help of God

Binah: Understanding; third highest of Ten *Sefiros*

Birrur: Separation; separation of good from bad

Chesed: Kindness; fourth highest of Ten *Sefiros*

Chiyah: Life; fourth highest of five soul levels

Chochmah: Wisdom; second highest of Ten *Sefiros*

Chutz L'Aretz: Outside the land (of Israel)

Drashah: Elucidation in presentation form

Drush: Exegetical; third level of *Pardes*

Emunas Chachamim: Faith in wise ones

Eretz Yisroel: Land of Israel

Erev Rav: Mixed Multitude; they left Egypt with the Jews

Gan Aiden: Garden of Eden

Gadol HaDor: Torah leader of the generation

Gedolim: Big Ones; leading Torah rabbis

Gematria: Number from adding value of Hebrew letters

Geonim: Great Ones

Geulah: Redemption

Gevurah: Strength; fifth highest of Ten *Sefiros*

Gehinom: Purgatory

Gilgulim: Reincarnations

GR"A: Acronym: Gaon Rebi Eliyahu (of Vilna)

Halachah: Torah Law

Halachic: Legal (according to Torah)

HaMelech: The king

Har Sinai: Mt. Sinai

Hashgochah Pratis: Personal (Divine) Providence

Hashkofic: Philosophical

Heichel: Sanctuary in the Temple before the Holy of Holies

Hod: Glory; eighth highest of Ten *Sefiros*

Inyan: Subject matter; issue

Ittah: Its time

Kabbalah: Esoteric area of Torah learning

Kanoy: Zealot

Kavshei Rachmanah: Secrets of the Merciful One (God)

Keitz: End; designated end of history

Keitz HaYomim: End of days

Kena'os: Zealousness

Keser: Crown; highest of Ten *Sefiros*

Kesones Ohr: Clothing of light (with an *aleph*)

Kesones Ohr: Clothing of skin (with an *ayin*)

Kesuvah: Marriage contract

Kibbutz Golios: Ingathering of the Exiles

Kinah: Jealousy

Klipah: Peel; Kabbalistically, spiritual impositions

K'nesses Yisroel: Assembly of Israel

Luchos: Tablets, as in the Ten Commandments

Malchus: Kingdom; tenth of Ten *Sefiros*

Manna: Heavenly bread of the 40 years in the desert

Maskilim: Intellectual ones

Midrash: Elucidated teaching; Oral Law story

Mikrah: Reading; the Written Law

Mishnah: Oral Law teachings

Mitzvos: Commandments

Moed: Appointed Time; Jewish holidays

Moshiach: Messiah

Moshiach Ben Dovid: Messiah, son of David

Moshiach Ben Yosef: Messiah, son of Yosef

Motzei: Goes out, as in when *Shmittah* year ends

Nachash: Snake; reference to the Original Snake in *Gan Aiden*

Nefesh: Rest; lowest of five soul levels

Neshamah: Breath: third highest of five soul levels

Neshikah: Divine kiss; death directly by God

Netzach: Dominance; seventh highest of Ten *Sefiros*

Nistar: Hidden (esoteric Torah)

Nukvah: Female; another name for the *Malchus*

Olam HaBah: World-to-Come

Olam HaZeh: This World

Pardes: Orchard; reference to four levels of Torah learning

Parshah: Section; weekly Torah portion

Posuk: Verse (from the Torah)

Pshat: Simple, as in the simplest explanation of an idea

Rabbeinu: Our teacher

Rambam: Acronym: Rabbi Moshe ben Maimon(ides)

Ramban: Acronym: Rabbi Moshe ben Nachman(ides)

Ramchal: Acronym: Rabbi Moshe Chaim Luzzatto

Remez: Hint; the second level of understanding of *Pardes*

Rishonim: First Ones

Ruach: Wind; second highest of five soul levels

Sanhedrin: Torah High Court

Satan: Obstructing (Angel)

Sefirah: Spiritual emanation; filter for God's Light

Sefiros: Plural of *sefirah;* there are 10 altogether

Shema: Hear (O Israel, the Lord our God, the Lord is One)

Shmittah: Let go; year land lays fallow in Israel

Shemonah Esrai: Eighteen (blessing prayer said daily)

Shvi'is: Seventh, as in seventh year of *Shmittah*

cycle

Siddur: Prayer book

Sitra Achra: Other Side; name given to the Obstructing Angel

Sod: Mystery; reference to Kabbalah

Talmidei Chachamim: Wise students; Torah scholars

Talmud: Volumes of elucidation of the Mishnah

Tanach: Acronym: *Torah, Nevi'im* (Prophets), *Kesuvim* (Writings)

Techiyas HaMeisim: Resurrection of the Dead

Teshuvah: Repentance

Tifferes: Harmony; sixth highest of Ten *Sefiros*

Tikun: Rectification

Torah: Five books of Moshe

Toras: An area of Torah learning, as in *Toras Moshiach*

Tzaddikim: Righteous people

Tzion: Zion

Yechidah: Single; highest of five soul levels

Yemos HaMoshiach: Days of *Moshiach*

Yerushalayim: Jerusalem

Yeshivah: Place of Torah study

Yesod: Foundation; ninth highest of Ten *Sefiros*

Yetzer Hara: Evil Inclination

Yetzer Tov: Good Inclination

Yetzirah: Formation; third highest of four "worlds"

Yiddishkeit: Judaism (in Yiddish)

Yishuv: Settlement

Zehr Anpin: Small Face; grouping of *Chesed* through *Yesod*

Zt"l: Remember the righteous one for blessing

Zuhama: Spiritual impurity for the First Snake

THE FOLLOWING are all the books written over the years. Some books may no longer be in print, but many are still available in either PDF or Kindle formats. Visit the Thirtysix.org OnLine Bookstore, or Amazon for more information, or to order online.

The Unbroken Chain of Jewish Tradition, 1985
The Eternal Link, 1990
If Only I Were Wealthy, 1992
If Only I Understood Why, 1993
If Only I Could See the Forest, 1993
If Only I Could Stay, 1993
If Only Great Was Greater, 1993
The Y Factor, 1994

Life's A Thrill, 1994
No Atheists in a Foxhole, 1994
Changes that Last Forever, 1994
The Making of a Great Jewish Leader, 1994
Bereishis: A Beginning With No End, 1994
The Wonderful World of Thirtysix, 1995
Redemption to Redemption, 1997
The Big Picture, 1998
Perceptions, 1998
Not Just Another Scenario, 2001
At The Threshold, 2001
Anticipating Redemption, 2002
Sha'ar HaGilgulim, 2002
Hadran (Hebrew), 2004
Talking About The End of Days, 2005
Talking About Eretz Yisroel, 2005
The Physics of Kabbalah, 2006
Be Positive, 2007
Geulah b'Rachamim, 2007
God.calm, 2007
Just Passing Through, 2007
On The Same Page, 2007
The Equation of Life, 2007
No Such Victim, 2009
Survival in 10 Easy Steps, 2009
Not Just Another Scenario 2, 2011
All In Your Mind, 2011
The Light of Thirtysix, 2011

The Last Exile, 2011
Drowning in Pshat, 2012
Drown No More, 2012
Shas Man, 2013
The Mystery of Jewish History, 2013
Survival Guide For the End-of-Days, 2013
Deeper Perceptions, 2013
Chanukah Lite, 2015
The Hitchhiker's Guide to Armageddon, 2016
Purim Lite, 2016
Pesach Lite, 2016
The Torah Empowerment Seminar, 2016
Siman Tov (Hebrew), 2016
The Fabric of Reality, 2016
Addendum, 2016
Fundamentals of Reincarnation, 2017
Reincarnation Clarified, 2016
All About Energy, 2017
What Goes Around, 2017
The God Experience, 2017
What in Heaven, 2017
The God Experience, Part 2, 2017
The God Experience, Part 3, 2017
It's About Time, 2017
Need to Know, 2017
Perceptions, Volume 2, 2017
Once Revealed, Twice Concealed, 2017
The Art of Chayn, 2017

A Matter of Laugh or Death, 2018
Geulah b'Rachamim Program, V. 1, 2018
Geulah b'Rachamim Program, V. 2, 2018
Geulah b'Rachamim Program, V. 3, 2018
Point of Acceptance, 2018
See Ya, 2018
In Discussion: Bereishis, 2018
Reincarnation Again, 2018
A Separate Matter, 2018
In Discussion: Shemos, 2019
A Search for Self, 2019
A Search for Trust, 2019
In Discussion: Bamidbar, 2019
How It Might Play Out, 2019
In Discussion: Vayikra, 2019
Where Are My Emotions Now, 2019
In Discussion: Devarim, 2019
The Early Years, 2019
Oh, So Blind, 2019
Not So Bad? 2019
Sha'ar HaPesukim: Shemos, 2019
The Fix, 2020
Sha'ar HaPesukim: Bereishis, 2020
Preparing For Redemption, 2020
Mindfulness, Torah & Redemption, 2020
Moment of Moments, 2020
My Zaidy's Diary, 2020
My Writing, Your Book, 2020

Living Higher, 2021

Any questions, especially regarding the dedication of an upcoming book, project, webinar, etc., should be sent to pinchasw@thirtysix.org.